Getting In, Getting Out!

A Journey from Chaos and Abuse To Love and Acceptance

by
Janis Watkins

authorHOUSE™

1663 LIBERTY DRIVE, SUITE 200
BLOOMINGTON, INDIANA 47403
(800) 839-8640
WWW.AUTHORHOUSE.COM

First published by AuthorHouse 09/06/05

ISBN: 1-4208-7393-8 (sc)

Printed in the United States of America
Bloomington, Indiana

This book is printed on acid-free paper.

Scripture quotations marked NIV are taken from the Holy Bible: New International Version®. NIV®. Copyright© 1973, 1978, 1984 by International Bible Society. Used by permission of Zondervan Publishing House. All rights reserved.

Scripture quotations marked TLB are taken from The Living Bible copyright © 1971. Used by permission of Tyndale House Publishers. Inc., Wheaton, Illinois 60189 All rights reserved.

Scripture quotations marked NLT are taken from the Holy Bible, New Living Translation, copyright © 1996. Used by permission of Tyndale House Publishers. Inc., Wheaton, Illinois 60189 All rights reserved.

Scripture quotations marked BBE are taken from the Bible in Basic English, © 1949, 1962 by C. K. Ogden and Cambridge University Press.

Cover design by Tina Weiss, Murals and More, St. Louis, Missouri

Author photo by Kellie Goodrich, Kellie Goodrich Photography, Fisk, Missouri, www.kelliegoodrich.com

This book is dedicated to Fern and Cathy who continuously pointed me to HIM and tirelessly prayed for me; Debra for encouraging me to write my thoughts and experiences; Penny who never once gave up on me; Barb who allowed me to heal at my own pace in my new home and Michelle for helping me learn how to laugh again!

A special thank you goes to Sheryl and Jeanette for their looking over every letter and lovingly correcting my errors. Thank you for not using red ink.

Endorsements

Getting In, Getting Out, though unique in detail to Janis Watkins' experience, is nevertheless applicable to thousands upon thousands struggling to "get out." Having known Janis when she was in her "living hell," I was just as duped as the rest of her family and friends. But God gave her the courage to get out, and she immediately knew she *must* share what the Lord has done. If you or someone you know is living a lie and paralyzed with fear to get out, Janis' personal walk gives a pattern for others to begin the process. I pray that as she has allowed the power of God's Word and the Holy Spirit to transform every aspect of her life, she can now bring hope and inspiration through this powerful book to those who need it desperately.

Dr. Debra Peppers
University professor/radio talk show host
St. Louis, Missouri

I have known Janis Watkins for several years. I first came to know her when she attended a class I was teaching for lay counseling training. During that year, I came to know her, and felt she had some walls, not knowing her background. I witnessed a transformation in Janis that was a testimony of what Jesus Christ can do in a person's life if they are open to His love and delivering power. *Getting In, Getting Out* is a book that will minister to anyone who has been through abusive relationships.

Dr. Mary Jo Schneller
Director of South County Christian Counseling,
and House of Restoration Lay Counseling
St. Louis, MO

Table of Contents

Foreword

Some people are molded on the potter's wheel, while others are forged in the blacksmith's shop. Those who are formed from clay certainly have a place, but those forged by the fire, the anvil and the hammer are a different breed. Those who have paid a high price to share their life lessons fall into a category of their own. They have weathered storms as well as barely survived some of the chapters of their life's story. There are some stories that need to be told because the survivors of these battlefields come away decorated with purple hearts and war medals. Their stories inspire and give hope. The story you are about to read leaves a trail of breadcrumbs for people in hopeless situations. It is truly inspirational but doesn't stop there; it gives a road map to victory. The hope given by *Getting In, Getting Out*, is that no matter how grave your circumstances may be, God can make a way where there seemingly is no way. When I read Janis' manuscript, I couldn't put it down. It is one of those books that is a must read for anyone who is tired of living in fear and is ready to declare their own freedom! Get ready to walk down a road of emotions as you read this inspiring story of hope, overcoming and victory. If you are one of those weary travelers looking for a way out, Janis has left tearstains in the sand for you to follow. This path is traveled by few, but for those who dare to go the distance, this trail of tears is there to lead you safely home.

Dr. Bryan Cutshall
Senior Pastor
Twin Rivers Worship Center
St. Louis, MO

Part One: Getting In

Dear Friends, now we are children of God
and what we will be has not yet been made known.
John 3:2 (NIV)

Chapter One: The Perfect Match

*This is now bone of my bone
and flesh of my flesh.
Genesis 2:23 (NIV)*

I was 32 years old when I married the man of my dreams. I had saved myself for just the right man with whom I could spend the rest of my life. Little did I know of the ride I would have during the next four years. I had not been actively looking for a husband. I had dated in the past, but never met Mr. Wonderful. I had an excellent job as an educated professional, which allowed me to support myself. I was active in my church and was enjoying life, as I knew it.

But then entered Joe (fictitious name), a very charming, good-looking man. We met in church, the ideal place to meet the man of your dreams. I sang in the choir and he spotted me from the congregation. He was a man of faith, active in the church and even joined the choir to meet me. I was swept off my feet to say the least. We had a wonderful time dating and Joe was always the perfect gentleman, my prince charming. We laughed at all the same things and had many hobbies in common. We went to movies, shopping, out to eat, everything couples do when they are getting to know one another. We even spent time praying together and reading the Bible. What an answer to prayer to have someone with whom I could share such a vital part of my life. He was so thoughtful in always bringing me flowers and little presents. He had just the right ways of letting me know he was thinking of me and that he cared. Joe would often call when we could not be together, and he encouraged me to do things with other ladies from the church. I did not question his sincerity. He always had a sweet smile when I was with him. We would hold hands as we walked and he liked when I put my arm around him whether in public or when we were alone. We were playful together and enjoyed showing each other affection.

Joe seemed to consider my opinions and choices to be of utmost importance to him. He would ask me how I felt about certain things that were happening in the world on both the local and global levels. I always tried to give my honest opinion and remain true to my convictions. We disagreed on very few issues. Since we both had a religious background, I believed we had the same beliefs and agreed on most things. All signs pointed to the fact that we were meant for each other. We both shared things from our pasts, our accomplishments and our defeats. I tried to be open and honest in every area of my past and believed that Joe had been as honest. That was not easy for either of us, but by that time, we were getting quite serious about each other and I knew the relationship was going to be something like I had never experienced before.

I had watched how Joe interacted with his family. I so desperately wanted to have a family of which I could feel a part . I saw how he treated his mother, which is supposed to be a good test of how a man treats other women. He was very respectful of her and always looked out for her and her feelings. He had a relationship with his father that many men would envy. They were both self employed and would often work together on larger jobs. They both enjoyed antiques and had a gift for spotting a good deal and a great antique. I was to find out later that this was a very superficial relationship. Still, his parents treated me like a daughter-in-law would love to be treated. I instantly had a place in their family and felt loved and accepted. I had never been close to my own mother, so a loving relationship with my mother-in-law to be was one I readily welcomed.

I was also able to become friends with Joe's sister. She was not overly close with Joe, but since she was always busy with her church, husband and two children, the lack of closeness usually went unnoticed. I relished the thought of having a niece and nephew. I had always wanted to be an aunt and now I was going to have the chance to be the best aunt ever. Her husband was also self-employed and often worked on jobs with Joe and his father. So everyone seemed like one big happy family. I was going to be so happy with all the changes that were coming my way. I was at a point in my life where I was ready for a change. I was enjoying my life, but a change that I felt God had brought to me was welcome.

Joe and I tried to do all the right things before we were married. We took part in premarital counseling, shared with each other's families and friends and spent time together ourselves. We went to church together, had fellowship with Christian couples, and were actively pursuing what God had for our new life together. We both had the same goals and ambitions and wanted God to be at the center of our pursuit of those. We wanted to care for each other, have children and raise them with the same Christian beliefs that were so important to us. Everything had fallen into place in such a way that I could not help but believe that God had sent this wonderful man to be my husband for the rest of my life. I felt God had given me the best gift ever: a mate to have and to hold and to serve Him with for as long as we both shall live.

So the wedding day finally came. The groom was handsome and the bride beautiful. Many of our friends and family came to wedding. I truly felt like a princess who was marrying her prince. Everyone was giving us his or her best wishes and love. I felt so blessed and knew God had answered my prayers for the opportunity to live happily ever after with my new husband.

We had the Hallelujah Chorus played after the minister presented us as husband and wife. It was a day of celebration and a day that would make every bride feel as if her dreams were coming true. A day of new beginnings and saying good-bye to things of the past as a new adventure waited with new expectations and surprises. But was I ready?

Chapter Two: The Beginning of My Mess

Children, obey your parents in everything,
for this pleases the Lord.
Colossians 3:20 (NIV)

Everything has a beginning, whether it is good or bad. And everything that happens in life is based on decisions and choices. I had made many choices in my life about how I viewed people and issues. Even though I had made a lot of those choices with a child's mind, I never saw the impact they had on my life. I was in a mess and did not even know it. I was in a mess before I ever entered my marriage to Joe. There were some things in my past that I had buried deep in my soul and I thought they were there to stay. I had lied to myself for years and did not even have a clue about the damage I had done to myself by harboring those lies. But I honestly didn't even know I had lied to myself. I had never dealt with some hurts and so by not dealing with them, I was lying to myself telling myself I was a whole, healed individual. But the wounds were still there. I did not know they had not healed but were festering underneath, waiting to spew their sickness all over my life.

My mess started when I was a young child. I had a fairly normal childhood.

My parents tried to provide my sister and me with everything they could and we never really wanted for anything. We were neither poor nor rich. We went on family vacations, had holidays with all the relatives, and did most normal family activities. But my family was dysfunctional on the inside and hid it well on the outside. My parents' generation did not air their dirty laundry. They never talked about family issues with anyone, including the family. They passed that damaging teaching to the next generation. I learned from an early age that many things were not discussed. We did not discuss feelings, money, sex, or family issues. In fact, there was no real communication about anything. Those were the rules. I do not blame my parents for those rules; they were just the rules for their time. But I learned the rules well and carried them with me. I learned that you do not argue with your parents or any adult and whatever they said was the way it was. Children were to be seen and not heard in those days. If you disobeyed or tried to reason or talk back, tempers were sure to fly and the child was told how bad they were for being disrespectful.

Often the stronger parent made the rules and many times that parent was not the father. My dad was very passive and seemed to allow my mother to make the rules, discipline the children, and make most of the family decisions. She had a strong personality and she very forcefully influenced our family. But as a child, I just learned to keep quiet and not cause any trouble. My sister was bolder than I was and I often saw the wrath of my mother shown to my sister in ways I knew I did not want to experience. I also knew I did not want to ever lose my temper because I saw the damage a bad temper could do. So, as a child, I made a conscious choice to not lose my temper. I even remember being in our kitchen at home and making that choice. I was not aware at the time, but I was shutting down a very healthy emotion that God had given me. I just did not know at that age that tempers were manageable. I had become my dad who never said much and went with the flow of about anything. If he spoke on family decisions or issues, I never saw or heard him. I learned to never address an issue and just let my mother say anything to me she wanted. I would only sit in silence and take whatever was said without any response. I had become the perfect little girl. Everyone always told me I was just like my dad. There turned out to be more truth to that statement than I realized.

There were many rules in our house growing up and I learned to obey them or suffer the consequences. Rules are necessary to teach discipline, not to instill fear into individuals. My sister and I learned do things on our own. My dad worked days and was up early and left before we were out of bed. My mom worked nights and so she did not get up with us in the mornings. We did not have a problem with her working nights, but we often found ourselves in trouble if she thought we were making too much noise. I learned to move very quietly as I made my breakfast and got myself ready for school. I did not want to hear how I was keeping her from getting her sleep. If we made too much noise, it seemed she thought we were intentionally trying to prevent her from sleeping. But my sister and I had to go in to see my mother in her room each morning before we left for school. We called it our "inspection." She would make comments about what we were wearing or how we had made too much noise. It seemed like to us that nothing was ever good enough.

We tried our best to please her, but we felt we were never able to satisfy her. We assumed we could not clean the house right, do the dishes right, dress right, or sometimes not even talk right. We both so desperately wanted to hear her say we had done a good job at something, but those comments were few and far between.

As I grew older, I began to see that my mother was not just that way with us in the home, but with people outside our home. Nothing ever appeared good enough at church, at a restaurant, a parking place at a store, a haircut, and the rest of the family. Many times I hated the ride home from church knowing it would be a constant onslaught of critical comments about people we had just seen. Either someone had said the wrong thing to her, ignored her, or they had sung a song she did not like or preached on the wrong topic. I did not understand how a person could talk badly about people after just coming from hearing the Word, but I knew I never wanted to do that. It turned out that the decisions I made to not be like my mom, I took to the extreme. I did not learn how to defend myself or even know that I had the right to do so. I chose to not lose my temper, talk back or complain even about the least little thing. I decided that my opinions and feelings were just that: mine. I was not willing to risk hurt from others if I expressed something someone did not agree with.

So I learned to live in fear of adults, especially dominating ones. I am sure in my mother's heart she truly wanted the best for us and she was not a bad mother; she herself was probably unhappy and her only way of dealing with her own pain was to make everyone else around her as miserable. That would lessen her pain. I do not think my mother even saw how unhappy she was. I am not even sure she realized how I felt as a child and I was not willing to tell her. And I don't think she had anyone she could talk with about how she felt. I do not remember my mother having many friends or at least friends for very long. I did not notice it at the time, but looking back, I can see things more clearly. She always seemed critical of my sister's friends and mine. I can see now that she might have been jealous of any relationships we had. It seemed as if she could not get past her pain to be happy for us. I was very close to my mother's sister when I was growing up and I don't think my mother did not like my having that relationship. I remember one incident where she denied being my mother. I was no longer living at home and had stopped by my aunt's house to visit with her. My mother was also there, but was out of the room when I arrived. When she came into the room where my aunt and I were sitting, my aunt said that her daughter was here for a visit. My mother proceeded to say that I was not her daughter. I was never quite sure what she meant by that because there was never any question of whom my parents were. But I remembered that she had said it. I guess she did not want to see the friendship I had with my aunt, knowing I did not have a friendship with her. My mother and aunt were never close so I assume it was perceived by my mother that I was choosing my aunt over her. That was never the case.

Another relationship I had that was very dear to me was with my friend Penny. We had gone to school together and enjoyed doing many things together. I spent quite a bit of time with Penny and her family. They seemed so much more normal than my family and not everyone was critical of everything. So with time, I guess my mother grew jealous of my relationship with Penny. My mother would make comments about my friendship with Penny and I tried to not let those comments bother me too much, because the friendship was one that I treasured.

Penny and I could go to church together, talk about God and then also act silly like girls do. Often my mother's comments would offend me and I had a feeling of anger inside of me. But I chose to never raise my voice, fight back, or even defend Penny or myself. I looked to my dad when my mother would make not so nice comments and he would never say anything. As a child, I did not understand his silence. I could only say to her that I was sorry she felt that way and leave the issues at that. It appeared to me that she was only trying to make my pain worse than hers. I had chosen to be a peacekeeper and not a peacemaker. I did not know how to say no to anyone or defend myself for fear of the consequences. I knew that I could just take whatever came my way and deal with how I felt about it later. I learned those lessons so well that they carried over into other areas of my life. When I needed to take a stand, I did not know how and that would only cause me more pain.

Chapter Three: Adding to My Mess

*No one is to approach any close relative
to have sexual relations.*
Leviticus 18:6 (NIV)

I had learned from my family to be submissive and take whatever came my way. We continued to do the normal family things on the outside and seemed to have a good time doing them. My family would often visit relatives out of town when I was a young girl, and the visits allowed my sister and me to play with some of our cousins we did not see everyday. I thought one of my cousins was so cool. He was older and had a motorcycle. I loved the sound it made and always wanted to go for a ride. So he would take my sister and me for rides together. Then he started to take us on rides separately. I liked riding separate at first because we could go faster and I enjoyed that. The thrills of the wind in my hair and the freedom of going nowhere were exhilarating. But the ride soon took a turn and went down a very unfamiliar road for me.

During the rides with just the two of us, he drove to a vacant place such as a construction site or the edge of some woods and he proceeded to put his hands on me in very inappropriate places over my clothes. At first, I tried to protest, but I was small in size compared to him and did not have much success. He told me that it was okay for him to touch me, we were family and that he would not do anything to harm me. And I knew what he was doing was wrong, but as a child who feared saying no to adults, I did not have in me the ability to stop him. My first incident with sexual abuse was his feeling over my clothes. But after he saw that I did not offer much resistance, he felt he could go further. So each time we went for a motorcycle ride, I knew something very uncomfortable was going to happen. I had said to my mother that I did not want to go riding anymore, but she thought that was foolish. I remember my dad saying I did not have to go if I did not want to, but my mother knew how much I loved rides and made me go. I do not think she knew why I did not want to go and she never asked. But since our family did not talk about sex and we did not argue with my mother, I felt I could not tell. Or if I did tell, it might be seen as my fault, and that could result in her losing her temper. I did not want any sort of scene, especially one that involved me and my mother. I could have also told another member of the family or friend of the family, but I knew anything I said would have been passed back to my mother. Since we appeared normal on the outside, I knew whomever I told would want to tell my parents and I was afraid of telling my mother. I was young and not capable of making adult decisions, but I suppose I subconsciously chose the abuse over having to discuss the issue with my mother. I chose not to trust my mother. So I continued to go for the rides and I continued to be sexually abused.

With each ride, the abuse would go a step further and soon he was putting his hands under my clothes and in my undergarments and rubbing his hand all over my chest and in my private areas. That happened several times and seemed to satisfy him. But not for long. The next step after that was for him to try and persuade me to touch him. Somehow, I managed to gather the strength to say no. Just the sight of him made me feel dirty and I did not want to touch any part of him. He did not try force me to touch him. He just went ahead and put his privates on me. I quietly cried and waited until he finished. I am very grateful to say that there was never ever any penetration, but the abuse was very real just the same and the scars I carried from those incidents were very deep. Thankfully our visits with this family grew less frequent and the cousin eventually moved out of his parent's house. I never told anyone about what had happened with my cousin and I have not seen him since the abuse.

As a child, I did not realize the impact these encounters would have on my life. I just prayed that I would forget them and move on with my life. I stored the memories deep inside hoping that they would never emerge. But all the while, they were seething and impacting my decisions and relationships. It was not until after I was married and divorced that I came to realize the effect they had on how I interacted with other people and how I viewed myself. There were many manifestations that became apparent as I grew older that now I know they were a result of the abuse. Not only did I choose not to trust my mother, I had a hideous sexual addiction that attached itself to me as a result of the sexual abuse. When I was a teenager, I often felt unloved or alone. I needed a way to try and feel loved. My home was not a nurturing environment and I needed encouragement at that stage in my life. I did not realize any of this at that time. I just knew there was something missing in my life and I was trying to fill the void in any way that I could. I did not even realize I had a problem. I used this crutch for many years and it became a regular part of my life. I never even thought of it as sin. It was simply something I used to help me forget my pain but all the while, it was keeping me in my crippled, pathetic mind-set and causing me more pain and injury. I was wounded, deceived and trying to go through life.

There were more results of the abuse that came to the surface, as I grew older. I had developed a distorted view of any intimate sexual relationship and I did not know it. I did not know how to show love or be loved. I did not realize that the thought of being intimate with a man was going to make me sick inside. From what I had been taught in church, I just knew that I was saving myself for marriage and never really thought about having sex. I had made the decision that sex outside of marriage was not an option for me. I had pushed my feelings from the abuse so deep and lied to myself about them ever influencing me. I went to church every Sunday, said my prayers, and paid my tithes. Surely old issues were removed during all that exposure to religion. My self-image was very poor. I had no self-confidence, but somehow managed to go through life with many successes in both college and my career. I never felt loved by anyone, not even God. I actually felt unworthy of love from anyone. I was able to always put on my smile and happy front. But I was so lonely inside. I see now that God had His hand on my life, but there were times that I even doubted if He knew where I was. So with all of this in me, I was now in the perfect relationship with everything I had ever dreamed of and it was all about to change. I was not in any shape to handle what was coming my way.

Chapter Four: Oddities of Joe

He fastens my feet in shackles;
he keeps close watch on all my paths.
Job 33:11 (NIV)

After meeting the love of my life in church, getting to know one another and making a commitment to one another till death do us part, I was on my way to the perfect life. Once the vows were said, the guests greeted, cake cut, and presents opened, the new life together began. It was an exciting time, a new life with the man of my dreams. I had dreamed of the day of new beginnings and now it had finally arrived. And what a day of new beginnings it was. It was a day of new beginnings that I would rather forget.

Following the wedding, we went on a Caribbean cruise for a week and then spent an additional week in Florida. Most of the times were good, but I became aware of a few oddities that my prince charming seemed to have. Joe had an issue with feet. He considered them to be filthy. Not his feet, but other people's feet. He mentioned it briefly to me while we were on the cruise and I tried to honor his few requests. Joe had asked me to please wash my feet after removing my socks and shoes. Now this did not seem necessary to me, but as a new wife, I was eager to please and was willing to oblige. Washing my hands after putting on or removing shoes and socks had not been a part of my normal routine while I was single. I viewed feet as being just another part of the body and not in any way dirty or disgusting. I worked very hard on making the washing a habit. So when I forgot, he raised his voice to a level I had not heard from him before and preceded to loudly tell me how bad I was for not remembering a simple request. I apologized and began to see a side of him I had never seen.

A second incident with feet occurred while we were in our hotel room in Florida. We had a beautiful room, right on the beach. We had gone into our room to get ready for an evening on the town. Joe had gone to take a shower and I was lying on the extra queen sized bed, reading. He had asked me to not lie on our bed and I agreed. So I lay on the spare bed, on my stomach with the book propped on a pillow. I had my head at the end of the bed and my feet at the top of the bed. Now, up to this point, his only request had been for me to wash my hands after removing my socks and shoes. But when he came out of the shower and saw me lying on the bed, with my feet at the head of the bed, he totally lost all control. I was ordered to get up, remove all the bed linens from the spare bed, including the comforter, and place them in the closet. I then had to take a shower to remove anything on me that might have touched the area where my feet had been. We then did not have any housekeeping for three days in our room. Joe knew the comforter and bed linens would just be put back on the bed without being laundered, and he could not deal with that thought. He was literally petrified of having those put back on the bed. And his anger toward me was something I had never experienced from another human being.

That was my first realization that he was not what he had portrayed himself to be. I felt as if I had been betrayed and sold a bad bill of goods. The issue with the feet would emerge many times throughout our marriage with the rules changing every time. The main goal of my honeymoon had become trying not to do anything that would anger Joe or set off his temper. But I realized that was not a realistic goal and was praying that things would be different when we returned home and settled into making our house a home. Joe had a very nice house in the beautiful neighborhood of an excellent school district, so we did not purchase a new house together. We were going home to "his" house.

When we returned from our two-week honeymoon, I was given the rules of the house. I had never dreamed of having to follow such rules in a marriage, rules set forth by the man of my dreams, rules that if they were broken, consequences were sure to follow. Rules so unbelievable to me that I honestly thought my husband was kidding. We had always joked around in the past and I prayed these rules were just part of a terrible joke. Well, I was soon to find out just how serious he was with his rules.

Chapter Five: The Rules.

Wives, submit to your husbands
as it is fitting in the Lord.
Colossians 3:18 (NIV)

The list of rules was long. They were too numerous for someone in shock to remember. I was in a daze, a somber sleep, praying to wake up and find the prince charming I had just married. Praying that he would say that he loved me, cherished me, and would take care of me forever, never mistreating me or hurting me in any way. He had been the perfect gentleman before we were married. He never raised his voice to me, was very attentive, and seemed to genuinely care about me. But I was soon to realize that my prince was gone forever.

The rules included not being allowed in the house by myself when Joe was not at home. Now that seems too far-fetched to believe, but it was true. I was given a key to the front door, but it was only for appearances. He left for work after I did and would lock the door from inside the house and I did not have a key to that lock. I was not allowed to have a garage door opener. He said there was really no reason for me to have one since he would always be home before me. I of course tried to reason with him, stating that there might be some days that I would need to come home before him. He emphatically let me know that would never be the case. He would always be home before me. So my visions of having dinner ready for my husband after his hard day at work were shattered. My idea of being a good wife in making preparations for a romantic evening with my husband was gone. How could I plan anything for him if I could not get in my own home? But I still seemed in a bit of a daze, not willing or able to believe what I was hearing from the man to whom I had just devoted the rest of my life.

But the rules got even more interesting and were constantly changing to fit his mood. On top of not being allowed in the house by myself, I was not allowed in any room of the house by myself, except for the bathroom. Anytime I wanted to go to another room, Joe would accuse me of wanting to be away from him or going to do something behind his back. He thought I did not want to spend time with him if I were leaving the room where he was. Or he would think that I was touching my feet or dropping something on the floor, which was where feet had been. I was to announce when I was going to the bathroom so he would be aware. I could not get up and get a drink without telling him. If he worked out in the garage, he set up a lawn chair for me to sit in while he worked. When he finished, we would go in the house together. His level of control on my every move was so intense.

I did try to reason with him and reassure him of my commitment to him. After all, wives are to submit to their husbands. But at the same time, it was reasonable for a wife to do things around the house while the husband does something else at the same time. That does not mean the love is over, it just means life is happening. But my reasoning was met with great resistance from him. The intensity of his anger would grow by the second. With my non-confrontational personality and always wanting to be a people pleaser, it was very difficult for me to argue with him. But then at times, even my not arguing with him would set off his temper. I thought about leaving a few times, but I had made a commitment before God that this was my one and only marriage. I had even told Joe before we were married that divorce was not an option for me. Ever!

I grew to dread coming home from work, not knowing what kind of mood Joe would be in when I arrived. I would have loved to have gone shopping after work to avoid him, but I was not allowed to go anywhere without him. Not even to the grocery store. If we went to the store, I came home first and then we went back out together. I never went back out by myself. If I even suggested going somewhere, he became a pathetic little boy asking me why I did not want to be around him. And if I were five minutes later coming home than he thought I should be, it was a barrage of name-calling and accusations. Even if I had been stuck in traffic that was reported on television, he still did not believe me and would accuse me of being up to something. There were times I begged him to call the local authorities to see whether or not I was telling the truth. He never would. He preferred to accuse his wife of lying.

I tried very hard to never lie to him about anything. I knew that would get me in worse trouble in the long run with him. But I was lying to everyone else and I did not like that. I felt I could not tell the truth to anyone. I either had to admit to the hell I was living in or lie to cover it. I chose to lie. There were several times in which Joe would call me at work, accusing me of something or wanting me to do something with him. He expected me to just leave and do whatever he wanted. He felt if I said I could not leave, then I was putting my work before him. He did not see that I had a responsibility to my boss and that I also was providing us with a steady income. So rather than have to explain that my husband was irrational about such issues, I often said I was sick and had to leave. The lying did make me sick, but at the time, I thought I had no other choice. I felt I had to obey him or suffer the consequences. Often I suffered the consequences even when I obeyed.

I recall one incident where Joe wanted me to leave work to go with him to our state capitol to purchase license plates for an antique car we owned. Rather than wait for the normal process of having the plates mailed to us, he wanted to go get them. I was at work and the capitol was a two-hour drive from there. Joe expected me to just leave what I was doing and go with him. If he were to go by himself, I would have been home before him and therefore waiting outside the house for him. That would not have looked good to the neighbors. I told him I could not just leave work on his command. That made him angry and he told me I better go with him and that he expected me at home within the hour. At that moment, I had to make a decision whether or not to obey him. I knew the results of not obeying, and I feared him. So I made up some sort of lie to leave. I was not happy when I arrived home and I told Joe that I was tired of lying at work in order to be meet his every command. That made him very angry. But I was also very angry. That was one of the rare times where I voiced my opinion. He made me drive that day and I recall him hitting me on the arm as I was driving. That hit was for one of the comments I made. I had obeyed him in coming home, but sharing my feelings about it just caused more grief and pain for me. That reinforced to me that I should not share my feelings with Joe.

Another incident involving one of the antique cars occurred when Joe had been working on one in the garage and asked me to take the key and put it in the usual place. I immediately obeyed and placed the key in the cup on a shelf near the kitchen sink. I had left the door to the garage open so he could see me as I put it away. A day or two passed and Joe wanted to start the old car, so he went to get the key. I cannot put into words the fear I felt when he did not find the key in that cup where I had placed it. I knew I was going to be blamed for it not being there, even though I had personally placed it there. He began to question me about the key and what I had done with it. I told him I had placed it there, but he chose not to believe me. I was terrified. I knew he had probably taken the key, but did not remember. I even suggested that. I do not remember the item he threw at me, but I remember being called evil names, names that a husband should never call his wife, names no one should even call another human being. We stayed up all night with his accusing me taking the key, questioning me about where I put it and what I was going to do with it. I again reminded him that I could do nothing with him always watching me and that he had even seen me put the key away. Neither one of us slept that night. I was afraid to go to sleep, not knowing if he would do something to me while I slept and he was too angry with me to sleep. The car seemed more precious to him than me.

My life was hell for the next few days. Joe was angry and was not afraid to let me know that. I was walking on eggshells, just hoping the key would appear.

I came home after a few days of living in fear, and Joe was in the garage, with the old car running. He had a smile on his face and seemed to be in a good mood. I was very cautious when I spoke to him and asked if he had found the key. He just smiled. He never told me where he found the key. I questioned him even months later and he never revealed where the key had been. In my heart, I know he must have taken it after I had put it away and he had not put it back himself. But Joe was never going to admit he had made a mistake. He preferred to blame his wife and then just enjoy his toy instead of being open and honest. I would have respected him if he had told the truth. Instead, I feared him and hated how he treated me even more. As a result of that occurrence, he watched me more and more.

I never had one moment to myself when I was at home. I could not talk on the phone without him being in the room. He then would always want me to tell something to whomever I was talking to. Mostly the comments were something pertaining to him; a job he was doing, a recent antique's purchase he had made, or some project he was working on. I would try to give him the phone so he could talk for himself, but that would only make him angry. I was not able to talk with Penny without him being right beside me, listening to my every word. He would make faces or soft comments about how I should hurry and hang up so I could be with him. Over time, it became such a struggle to carry on a normal conversation that I would say whatever I could to get off the phone quickly. I knew how odd it seemed to others to always have Joe right there when I was talking and my way of dealing with it was to totally remove myself from the chance of that happening. If I avoided the problem, I did not have to talk with anyone about it and then face the truth of how weird my marriage was. But a consequence of that decision was to not have contact with some of my oldest and dearest friends. I had hoped they would think Joe and I were so happily married that we wanted to spend every waking moment together. But I was only lying to others and myself as my marriage continued to fall apart.

The foot issue was getting more bizarre by the day. There was never a day while I was married to Joe that I was able to come home, kick off my shoes at the door, and relax. Shoes were not taken off until it was time to go to bed. In addition, he had started a routine of watching me dress and undress to make sure I did not touch my feet or let anything touch the floor. If I did, he would have an outpouring of his temper that would often result in his spitting on me and then throwing away the clothes I had on. I had to sleep with my hands under my pillow at night so that I would not touch my feet. There were many nights that Joe would wake up thinking I had touched my feet. That brought an immediate rage to our bedroom, even though I tried reassuring him that I could not possibly touch my feet while lying flat on my back. But he would proceed to hit me with a pillow, call me hideous names and make me get up and wash my hands. Then, after I would return to bed, I would have to hear about how I was causing him to lose precious sleep that he needed to be able to work the next day. I was in fear of him and did not have the guts to fight back.

The list of rules continued to grow. I was eventually told I could not touch anything in the house without first asking permission. Moving a glass on the dining room table while we were eating dinner would bring an onslaught of questions and accusations. Any movement was questioned and twisted to make it seem like I was trying to do something behind his back. I did not understand how he thought I could do something behind his back when he was always with me.

We had very few visitors in our home. Joe was so concerned about people touching items we had in the house that he could not even allow himself to enjoy other people's company. I often wanted to have his sister and her family over, but he thought their children might break something. He could not get past his "stuff" to allow people in his life. The few times we had visitors, he was very strained, but it appeared to others that he was being helpful and the perfect host. He waited on everyone for everything. His waiting on them was his way of controlling what they touched and where they went in the house. But I was still not let out of his sight. He would always ask me to assist him if he had gone into another room for something. I remember one time when my friend Penny came to spend the night with us. She and I did not have a moment to ourselves just to visit. The next morning, Joe wanted to go to the gas station to put gas in one of the vehicles. He wanted me to go with him. I protested to the point where he started to lose his temper. I did not want Penny to hear us fighting, so I went with him. I asked him on the way to the station why he thought he could trust my friend in the house alone but not his wife. I told him he should have been able to trust his wife more than anyone. That comment rendered a string of insults and names in my direction.

I was not allowed to see the mail. Joe would always open any mail addressed to me and then tell me what it was. If I even asked about the mail, that would set off a huge display of anger. I jokingly told him once that it was a felony to open someone else's mail. He did not see the humor in my comment. He insisted that he never threw out anything of mine. But with my not seeing the mail, I never knew for sure.

He controlled every day of my life. I was not allowed to stay at home when I was sick. I remember one time when I had to go to work with him. On that particular day, he was working in an apartment where there was no heat. I had a fever and it was very cold outside. I did not need to be anywhere except home. I did not even feel like going to work, which I would do when I did not feel well, just to get away from Joe. But that day, I was too sick even to go to work.

So I ended up sitting on the floor in a cold, vacant apartment. I remember just shivering and trying not to complain. I knew I did not need to be in that cold apartment, but if I were too sick to stay with him, we would go home and I would have to hear about how much money he was losing because of his having to stay at home with me. If he were staying with me at home, he was not working and therefore he was not making any money. When I was frozen and felt my temperature rising, I insisted that we go home. And as I had predicted, he complained all the way home and even when we arrived home. I reminded him that he had made the rules, not me. That was the wrong thing to say and resulted in my being spit on and hit on the arm.

I have to honestly say that in the beginning of the marriage, Joe and I had some fun times together, but always with the condition of things going his way. That was easy because I was in such a state of wanting to please, I only enabled him to have his way without any give or take or real communication. When he was in a good mood, he had a good sense of humor and was fun to be with. But there was always a part of me that was afraid to speak my mind or to cross him. At first I tried to be as open and honest about my opinions as I could, but he would make me feel as if what I said was unimportant and stupid. I gradually learned to say what I thought he wanted to hear. So his control of me continued to spread even to the way I thought and communicated.

Little did he know that the more he tried to control me, the more I did not want to be around him. He was killing my love for him by killing my spirit. I guess he could sense my fear of him and how cautious I had become around him and that made him want to try and control me even more. His fear of losing me was greater than his ability to love me. Joe so desperately needed love himself that he did not know how to love. And I was not able to receive any kind of love. I never thought I deserved it. We did not know how to give or receive love, and therefore the marriage deteriorated daily to the point where I was only focused on survival.

.

Chapter Six: Down Hill Fast

Listen to my cry for I am in a desperate need;
rescue me from those who pursue me
for they are too strong for me.
Psalm 142:6 (NIV)

Joe was a classic abuser in the sense that he knew when he had mistreated me. I would often come home to gifts or cards, all given with an apology. I had lived more than three years of apologies. That was his way of making things all right between us. I often told him I would have rather had him and me in a loving, respectful relationship than all the presents in the world.

I was beginning to shut down emotionally. I had shut so many people out of my life, not wanting anyone to know the hell I was experiencing. I was embarrassed that my life was in shambles. But I did not seem to be able to get off the downward spiral that my life was on. I lost interest in many things that in the past I had enjoyed. Fishing had become a chore and I could not even focus on football. Those lacks of interest should have been a sign to me, but I was in so much pain I did not notice. I was at the point that Joe could almost say or do anything to me and I would not show any emotion.

Physically and emotionally, I was exhausted. Lying to everyone and to myself on a daily basis was taking my life from me. I was tired of pretending to have the storybook marriage that everyone thought we had. From the outside looking in, we had the perfect life. Joe and I were always together, wearing new clothes, driving new cars, taking expensive trips, and I regularly would be showing off a new piece of jewelry given to me because he "loved me." The last piece of jewelry he gave me was for our anniversary. We had no money at the time and he had traded work for the ring. I insisted the ring was not necessary, given our financial status at the time. He said he had to give me something because he knew his parents would ask me what my anniversary present had been and I needed something to show. Quite a romantic thought. He was concerned more about what others thought of him than what he thought of himself or me.

Financially, we were drained. Joe was a very giving person, which has its place. I supported his giving to others. But he could not say no to himself, even to the extent of not paying bills in order to purchase cars, antiques, or any other thing he thought he could not live without. We would have many phone calls every evening from bill collectors, wanting their money. We were several months behind on our mortgage and once came close to losing the house. We had our phone turned off several times. That was almost a blessing. I was so very tired of lying to people. And Joe had to keep buying new phones because he would get so angry that he would beat them on the counter until they were destroyed. Our furnace had broken and we did not have the seventy-five dollars for the part needed to fix it, so we slept in a house in the middle of winter without any heat until he came up with the money to fix the furnace. There were many times that all we had for dinner was Chef-Boy-Ardee ravioli from a can. Joe had even suggested that I get a part time job in the evenings, while he sat at home. He could not have worked at night, because then what would I do? I certainly could not stay at home by myself without him! I went as far as place applications at my current place of employment for night positions. I knew taking a night job would be very difficult on me physically, but at the same time, it meant extra income and less time spent with Joe. The thought of a second job almost made me feel safe. But I never received a call for an interview and Joe had decided that my working in the evenings might be too difficult to explain. We had to do whatever we could to maintain the image that he thought was so important.

Joe's temper had progressed to the point that I literally was afraid to say or do anything, and he was becoming more public with his temper. There were several businesses that had asked us not to come back because of his display of emotions. He had cursed out waitresses, called people cleaning his car horrible names, and thrown objects across parking lots of car dealers while salespeople watched.

I called the police to the house one night when he was hitting me and throwing things at me. But by the time they arrived, he had calmed down, apologized, and promised to never do those things again. I was embarrassed to let the police know what my life was like, so I lied when they came to the door. Why did I lie when there was someone there who could help me? I honestly did not believe Joe when he apologized that night. He had given me those empty promises in the past. Yet, I was passing an opportunity for help. I think I was afraid that they would not believe me and they would leave and I would be left with Joe. I also thought that perhaps they could get me out that night, but that ultimately I would be returned there and have to face Joe. Either way, facing Joe and his wrath was at the end of any situation I could imagine.

Afterward, the police sat in their patrol car right outside the house for almost an hour. During that time, no words were spoken between Joe and me. We went to bed. But after they had pulled away, the hideous names began to flow from his mouth and he hit me with both his fists and his pillow. Joe thought using a pillow was not abuse. When it rams your head into the wall, it is abuse. But I evidently did not think the abuse was bad enough to leave.

I occasionally had a bruise on my arm where he had hit me or a bruise on my leg where he had thrown something at me. I knew it was not right, but did not think the bruises were a reason to leave. What would it take for me to leave? How much hitting, spitting, and controlling was I going to allow myself to take before I realized it was enough? As his temper grew worse, I think I either convinced myself or allowed him to convince me that it was my fault that he lost his temper. I took the blame for everything, even when I was not wrong, to try and avoid an argument or him losing his temper.

I never knew what would set off his temper. We could be eating dinner, I would say or not say something, it didn't really matter which, and he would proceed to throw a dish of food or some other object at me. I had learned to dodge flying objects quite well after four years. Then there was a mess to clean up and I was not allowed to do that. So, many times, dried food would still be on the floor days after he had put it there. The conditions of the house were becoming so unhealthy.

Joe refused to throw anything away and had newspapers and junk mail piled everywhere. Trash accumulated and he stashed it in places trash should not go. He had pizza boxes, empty cookie packages, newspapers, empty two-liter bottles, soiled paper towels, and many other items all stashed behind his recliner in the basement. The vacuum had broken and we did not have the money to have it fixed, so the floors were never cleaned. When I would try and talk with him about it, he would just say that he hoped I still loved him in spite of his faults. I told him I did, but wanted to live in a healthy environment. I tried to reason with him, hoping he would see that the way we were living was not healthy. He then would get angry and tell me that he worked hard all day and did not feel like cleaning when he got home. I volunteered to clean, but that resulted in severe name-calling and small pieces of furniture being thrown at me. Whatever was closest to him was what I had coming my way.

There were many times when Joe would lose his temper and I honestly did not know how to respond. In those times, I would often just cry. I was not able to express my anger because I did not know how, and I also feared how Joe would react to my getting angry. What if my losing my temper caused him to react even more violently than he already had? I was not sure how far he would go with his physical and verbal assaults, and I did not want to find out. So I simply cried. But even that small showing of emotion would upset Joe. Not to the point of remorse, but to the point of calling me a big baby and accusing me of not taking things like an adult. He told me how silly it was for a woman in her thirties to be crying. His response to my tears just reinforced that he did not care about me or my feelings and that in turn caused me to shut down my emotions even more.

Intimacy with Joe had become a nightmare. I can honestly say that I was terrified. My only sexual encounters in the past had been with my cousin and I had shared those with Joe. I assured him before we were married that I had dealt with my issues from that abuse and I honestly thought I had. I was so wrong. My way of dealing with them had been to not talk about them with anyone, not think about them and just pretend they had never really happened. But they had happened and I was bringing all my hurt and mixed up emotions to our first time together. I must say that on our wedding night, Joe was very gentle with me. He knew I was a virgin and he wanted me to remember that night. But I was so sick on the inside. I put it off at the time to the fact that I was just nervous. But it was more than that. I felt like I was doing something filthy and sinful. But I went through the motions and tried to please Joe. I would do whatever act he liked, and just like my previous abuser, that satisfied him for a while. But there were certain things I had requested Joe not do, because those acts had been done to me. Eventually, Joe thought if he performed those old acts, it would help me get over the pain and heal. Even at the time, I recognized his thinking as warped. His actions only caused more grief for me. It caused me to remember the incidents with my cousin even more vividly and feel the pain from those times. As time pasted in my relationship with Joe, I grew to hate being intimate with him.

As time went by, Joe used sex to punish and control me. In one instance, my aunt and uncle had come to town and I was to take them to the airport the next morning. For me not to take them would have raised too many questions that Joe would have had to answer, so I was allowed to take them. While I was waiting for them to get ready, I was putting on my shoes. Joe thought I touched the doorknob to the door of our bedroom on the way to wash my hands. It did not matter that I had not touched it; he thought I did. I was very angry inside. Not only was he accusing me of something I had not done, he was choosing to make an issue of it while my family was in the house. He accused me of lying to him and I told him as quietly as I could that I had not touched the doorknob and that I had nothing to lie about. He still did not believe me and felt he had enough reason for him to spit on me and call me names.

But that morning, in addition to those abuses, he told me I better return home after stopping at the airport and not go straight to work. My going to work had been the original plan. I was torn between going to work and going back home. But I had such fear of Joe that I was afraid of what he would do to me when I came home that evening. I had seen Joe at what I hoped could only be his worst, but deep down inside, I knew he could take his abuse to another level. That fear was what I allowed him to use to keep control over me. So I went back home after sending my aunt and uncle on their trip.

That was the first time I actually felt like I had been raped. Joe was very forceful and threw me on the bed, tore off my clothes, and forced himself on me. All the time, he was calling me names and telling my how I better not be disobedient again. I was so angry inside, but did not have a healthy way to show that. I felt so humiliated and worthless. When he was finished, he told me to put my clothes on and go to work. I told him I felt like he had just raped me. He laughed and told me a husband could not rape a wife. It was not rape if the two people were married. He could think what he wanted, but I knew I had just been treated in a way no human being ever deserved. There were other times that he was very forceful with me or used sex to try and teach me a lesson. Each time I just prayed that he would finish quickly. I prayed a lot of times just to make it through a day.

Spiritually, I was famished. Joe and I only went to church when he wanted to go or did not have something else he wanted to do. We certainly did not attend on a regular basis and I was not allowed to go by myself. I guess he thought I might talk about him and about our life. I was only interested in going to church to worship the Lord and not talk about my life with my husband. Before I was married, I had always attended church regularly and was active in several ministries. But after I married, I was starving for spiritual food. I could not even have a few minutes each day alone to read my Bible. That was considered taking time from us as a couple. The only time I had to myself was on my twenty-minute drive to work. I learned to pray fast. At the beginning of the marriage, I was praying for God to change me so that I could be the wife Joe needed. Next my prayers revolved to asking God to change my husband. Then finally, my prayers were for God to make a way for me to get out. I was not sure if God had allowed me to get in my mess so He could get the glory and show me the way out or if I had just put my self in the mess on my own. Either way, I needed His help.

For more than three years, I had never felt that I could leave Joe, even though many times I told myself I should. I was not secure enough in who I was to think I could leave. I did not feel good enough about myself to think I was worthy of having a better life. I had ultimately chosen the life I was living by staying. I felt unloved, but yet some sort of bizarre security in staying with Joe. I had a room over my head, clothes on my back, and a secure job. I think I perceived the abuse of Joe as love. I so desperately wanted to feel loved and any attention felt like love to me at that stage of my life. I had proven to myself that I could handle any abuse that Joe might chose to send my way. I had been strong enough to stay in the marriage for that length of time and survived. I had stayed because the verbal, mental, and physical abuse had become such a way of life for me. I had forgotten how to live. Decisions were made for me each and every day and I did not have to think about my life or how I was living. I had become so shutdown I was at a place where I had to either resign myself to that life of hell forever or get out. I had reached the point where I was not concerned about what people thought; I was just not capable of making the decision to leave. I prayed for God to either make it so bad, that I had to leave, or give me the strength to stay in the marriage.

Chapter Seven: The End Is Near

The Lord is close to the brokenhearted
and saves those who are crushed in spirit.
Psalm 34:18 (NIV)

The weekend before our fourth anniversary was a turning point for me in our relationship. It was at that time I had only fear of my husband. The love was dead. It had been slowly dying, but on that particular weekend, the love was finally laid to rest.

Joe got mad because I let one of the two English bulldogs we owned near the couch in the basement. Now granted he had asked me to not let them get near there, but at the same time, I was up changing the channel on the TV for him. (He had smashed the remote a long time ago) So he got mad, kicked the dogs across the room, and forced me to go take a shower. What my taking a shower had to do with anything, I did not know. But it was time away from him, so I was glad to go. I was not feeling any emotion at that point. I obediently got in the shower, enjoying not being near him. I was not angry, upset, or even afraid. I am not saying I was at peace with what was going on, but all my emotions lay comatose. I felt absolutely nothing except total mental and physical exhaustion.

While I was in the shower, he threw a flip-top daily calendar from the bathroom over into the shower on top of me. I guess he was angry and that was the closest thing he could put his hands on to throw at me. I calmly and without thinking, tossed it back over the shower curtain. I was tired of dealing with his childish ways and did not want to play anymore. The calendar landed on the floor. That resulted in my being called many names, but nothing different from what I had experienced in the past. I still continued to feel nothing. I let the water wash away what I was experiencing.

Then I heard what sounded like glass rattling. (I was not allowed to look out of the shower without permission) He then told me to look. He had taken between $300-400 worth of perfumes and thrown them into the trash. Ninety-five percent of them were Christmas gifts from other people. I said fine, in a dead voice, and closed the shower curtain. Then flying over into the shower came a picture of my mom and dad (they had it nicely framed, and given it to me for my birthday.) He had taken it out of the frame, ripped it into several pieces and pitched it in the shower with me. Still, I did not feel any emotion. At that point, he could have done anything to me and I would not have even felt it.

He then told me I could get out of the shower. While I was drying off, (of course I was watched to make sure I didn't touch my feet or let the towel touch the floor) he took my grandfather's antique pocket watch and literally ripped the front and back metal covers off. That was the only thing I had from my grandfather. And it was very precious to me. I did not even try to calm him down. I just let him go. I was beyond the point of caring about him or caring about what he might do to me. I knew I could survive anything he did to me. I did not even feel hate towards him for what he had done. My emotions were not registering. I did not even think about leaving him at that point. I was not thinking anything. He was so out of control. He threatened to hit me, and I told him if he did, I was calling the police. And I think he knew I would do it since I had in the past. But I am not sure I would have been thinking or caring enough about myself to call the police.

The following weekend, which would be the weekend following our anniversary, we went to a town near ours for a night. We had won a stay at the Holiday Inn there. That was all we were doing, since we didn't have a dime to our name. But while we were there, I was getting undressed and supposedly sat where someone may have had his or her feet on the bed. I had sat on the end of beds before but somehow it was different on that occasion. Joe went ballistic. I had to take a shower, and then I had to get either another room, because he was not staying in that one, or we were going home. I said home was fine with me, but he wanted to stay. So I lied to the clerk about something being wrong in the room and somehow managed to get another room. I was so sick of lying for him. I was physically getting sick from all of the lies. I could not remember the last good night's sleep I had.

I knew that I probably should have left a long time ago. But like so many other women out there, I thought he would change. I had hoped that he would realize that we needed help and that he would be willing for us to get that help. But I had reached the conclusion that Joe was not going to change. But someone said to me once, God can change any person, but that person has to want it and has to ask for it. It was becoming very clear Joe was not asking. I had offered many times to go to counseling by myself if he thought it would help our relationship. I had asked once about the both of us attending sessions, but that was met with strong opposition and I quickly learned not to ask that again.

It was as if Joe were trying to destroy anything that might make me happy so I would be as miserable as he. I was at a total loss as for what to do next. I was just praying that God would protect me and that we could go to church on Sunday. I so desperately needed to hear from God. I prayed that He would not disappoint me.

Part Two: Getting Out

*Turn to me and be gracious to me for I am lonely and afflicted.
The troubles of my heart have multiplied; free me from my
anguish.*

Psalm 25:16-17 (NIV)

Chapter Eight: RELEASED!

*An ever present help
in time of trouble.
Psalm 46:1 (NIV)*

I knew I was finished with the relationship. My life was in a mess and I needed to find a way out. Somehow I had mustered enough courage to think about leaving. I had never really thought that I did not deserve the abuse from Joe. It had just become a way of life for me. I did not have the ability to stand up for myself and I took whatever behavior he displayed regardless of how wrong or painful. I had shut down emotionally and had excluded so many people from my life. I had no interest in anything and was simply going through motions at work and at home. I no longer had any feeling for my husband except fear. But I still needed to feel like I was released. This is something I cannot explain. I think if someone has been in an abusive relationship, they will understand that feeling. Because I had been under such a controlling person, I felt I needed permission to leave. I had needed permission to do anything for the past four years. I felt God was the only one who could grant me permission for such a bold move.

The next Sunday came and Joe was in a very good mood, so we were going to church. I was so thankful. It was a rare occasion for him to be both in a good mood and willing to go to church. When it came time for the pastor to speak, I was not thrilled with his message title, "I've Got Confidence." [1] I had been lying to myself all these years and thought that I had plenty of confidence and there was not going to be anything in that sermon for me. So I sat next to Joe, waiting for the sermon to end so I could get back to my hell. But the pastor started making statements that were hitting home with me. He said that some people there that day were in conflict or distress. I was able to relate to the feeling of distress. He went on to say that we should never let anyone cheat us from being ourselves. I began to listen more intently. I knew I was shutting down emotionally and I knew Joe was stealing my identity from me. I had let his criticism, sarcasm, and judgementalism take control of my emotions. The pastor said another person's sour mouth and attitude could ruin my life. Others often set up rules that they expect everyone else to live by. Now I felt like he was talking to me. Joe had set rules and expected me to follow them or suffer the consequences and he did have a sour mouth and attitude.

But it was the pastor's next comment that penetrated the wall of defense I had built around myself. He simply stated that he did not know whom the statement was for, but there was nothing stupid or ugly about me. I KNEW that was for me. Joe had often told me how stupid I was, or how ugly I was, or how horrible I looked in an outfit. I never was able to do anything good enough to please him or able to look good enough for him to compliment me. But the pastor had also mentioned there was nothing disgusting about me. God had created me the way I was and I was celebrated in heaven. Joe had always considered my feet disgusting and never had a problem sharing that with me. But I knew they were not disgusting. No part of me was disgusting. I was needing someone to tell me that and my pastor had. He said that when you know something is bad, you can stop it and you must stop it. I knew at that moment that I was free to leave Joe. It was as if God had said I was free to go. I had let Joe run over me. There was a difference between being passive and being peaceful. I had been very passive and let Joe take from me who I was.

I had a hard time remaining in my seat that day. But I realized if I had any kind of outward reaction to the pastor's words, Joe would question me. I sat very still even though I wanted to shout to the top of my lungs that I was free from the shackles I had allowed Joe to put on me. I no longer had to be called names, hit, spit on, or controlled. I was feeling a level of confidence I had never felt before. I knew I needed to start believing in myself and who I was in God. I had to believe in what God had put inside me. There was a purpose for my life and no other person could complete my purpose. I was uniquely created. So no matter what Joe said to me or about me, I was getting a glimpse of how God saw me. No human being deserved treatment like how I had allowed Joe to treat me. God never intended for marriage to be a controlling or abusive relationship and I was leaving!! I did not know how I would leave, when I would leave, or where I would go. But I knew I had been released and I was not going to stay any longer than I had to.

Chapter Nine: The Plan

But everything should be done
in a fitting and orderly fashion.
1 Corinthians 14:40 (NIV)

Since I knew I had been released from my bad marriage, I had peace about making plans to leave Joe. I had to do everything in secret. I had to make sure I stayed in my "normal" routine and did nothing that would make him suspect my intention. If he found out about my plan, I was sure the price I would have had to pay would have been great. But I knew I was doing the right thing and at that point, there was no turning back. I actually already felt free. Up to that time, I had never lied to Joe about anything I was doing at work or to and from work. But after feeling released, I had to do things that Joe did not need to know. I prayed that God would protect me and give me favor.

Since no one knew the truth of my marriage, I had to confide in someone and ask for help. I would not be able to leave Joe on my own. I first contacted my best friend, Penny. I had known her for many years. We had shared many years of our lives together prior to my marriage, so I felt I could trust her with one of my darkest secrets. I also knew she would not judge me or want me to explain why I was leaving. In the past, I had seen her to be a person of action when people had been in trouble and I knew she would do the same for her best friend. While I was married, I had never been able to have a conversation with her without Joe being in the same room. I would occasionally call her from work, but I always felt like I was going to get caught by Joe, so those calls were very infrequent. But I called Penny and told her I needed to meet with her and asked her to come to my work. It was a miracle that she was going to be in town the very next day. God was already working in my favor. It was a rare occasion for Penny to be in town. She agreed to pick me up for lunch. I told Joe I was going to be attending a seminar. He very rarely questioned anything that had to do with my work. By that time in the marriage, he knew how desperately we needed my income and he did not want to jeopardize that source.

Penny picked me up at my work and we drove to lunch. I spent a good part of the time trying to think about what would be the best way to tell her about my marriage. I waited until after we had eaten and were in the car. I had typed a list of all the rules in my life and the behaviors of Joe. I simply gave her the list and asked her to read it. Her reaction was one of controlled anger and wanting to act. She revealed to me that she was not shocked and had suspected my marriage was not the ideal one that Joe and I tried to portray. She was just surprised at the extent of his control and abuse. But she agreed to do whatever I asked. I told her I was developing a plan and needed her help to follow my plan through. She took me back to the lab. I waited for Joe to call to see if my "seminar" was over, and then went about my day as if I had never talked with Penny.

Penny was my dearest and most trusted friend, but I also needed a few people who were in the same town as me to help me. I contacted two women from my church that I felt I could trust. I had worked with them in an area of a ministry in the church, which required confidentiality. I had never heard them talk about other people or divulge secrets outside the walls of the ministry. I knew whomever I told would have to protect both my secret and me. I decided the best way to tell people were through letters. That way, they could absorb the information they were reading at their own pace and they could also decide if they wanted to be a part of the help I needed. So I wrote letters and sent them. I then waited. Both women contacted me and offered whatever help I needed. I was very thankful. They were both shocked, but willing to help me get out of my terrible mess. One of them asked if they could share my story with our pastor. I agreed. If I could not trust the pastor, I was in big trouble. He was shocked and called me at work, offering me support and prayers. He asked if he could contact someone to find out some information regarding Joe's bizarre behavior. I agreed. We both were flabbergasted when we received her response. The professional stated that the situation I was in was abuse plain and simple. She said that Joe had a mixture of symptoms and distorted thinking. It was her judgment that I would never be able to help him and that I should not remain in the situation. To her, Joe sounded very dangerous. My pastor gave me some information about an abused woman's center that was divinely located in a building very close to mine. I was able to contact them and Joe never knew. They worked around my lunch schedule when I knew Joe would not call. The people there were very supportive. They did not tell me what to do; they only looked over my ideas and offered advice.

I spent a great deal of time developing my plan to leave Joe. I knew everything had to be organized. I also knew I would have to recruit help. I had to be so careful in telling people. I decided on a date to leave. My paycheck was automatically deposited into our checking account. I could have the process stopped through my employer and Joe would never know it. So I took care of that first. I knew once that was secured, there was no turning back. I then asked Cathy, one of the ladies from church whom I had written about my situation, if she would help me move. She quickly agreed. I knew she had been praying for my safety and ability to make good decisions.

I was going to have to accomplish all my moving goals from work. I also knew I would not get much work done during this time. But I did not want any of my coworkers to know what I was doing. I did not want Joe to call and someone accidentally say something to him and give away my secret. So I decided to tell my boss and our secretary. I informed them of my life with Joe and they were extremely supportive and agreed to help me in any way they could. I was thankful that my boss was so understanding and more concerned about my safety than the work I would not be doing. That was a blessing. I informed only one of my coworkers whom I had known for many years, Jonathon, of my plans and he agreed to store moving boxes for me. He was going to be moving himself soon, so it was the perfect cover. He also agreed to help me move. I knew I would need some strong men to help me that day. And I also wanted a few men with me just in case something went wrong and Joe showed up during my escape.

I told Penny of the date and she cleared her calendar for that date. I mailed my parents a letter about one week before the move date informing them of my life and current plans. I needed someone to arrange for a moving truck and I also needed a temporary place to store some of my things. I did not want to tell them too soon and put them in a position to lie or act differently toward Joe if they happened to see him. I was not sure I trusted them to not react if they saw Joe after they knew the truth about our marriage. So I felt the least amount of information they had at the latest date was the best. My parents called me at work after they had read their letter. They both said they had known things were not right in the marriage, but did not realize the extent of how bad it was. They agreed to get a truck and meet whenever I was ready.

I spent much of each day at work going over my plan. I would not be able to take things out of the house prior to the day of moving. Joe noticed every little detail in the house and anything out of the ordinary sent him into a sea of rage. I recall one incident before I had been released to leave him, when he phoned me at work asking me why a certain window blind in the guest room was open. He was accusing me of having opened it behind his back. I pointed out to him that the window was in a room that I was not allowed in by myself so I would not have been in there and that I did not really care if the blind was open or not. He then decided that I had gotten up in the middle of the night and walked into that room with my bare feet, and opened the blind. Well, in his mind, I had broken many rules and that brought on an entirely different set of accusations. He proceeded to barrage me with names and threats of how we would pursue the issue when I got home. I dreaded going home that night. When I arrived, he called me every name in the book, threw stuff at me, and told me he would have to watch me now more than ever since I could not be trusted.

So from work, I had to decide what I wanted to take with me when I left. I really only wanted to take my clothes, personal items, and any wedding gifts that were from people I knew. So many things had been broken and that made me sad, but I realized that I was getting out of a horrible situation and material items did not really matter. I tried to look around a room at night, whatever room Joe and I were in, and make a note of what I wanted from that room. Then the next day at work, I wrote those items on the list. I managed to go through the whole house, except for one room, in a matter of a few weeks. I divided the rooms of the house into groups and then teamed the people helping me move with those rooms. Each team had a room or two and a list of items to be taken from that room. I was extremely detailed. I wanted everyone to be able to get the items on their list without my supervision. I had to take care of packing my personal items that I would need over the next few days. And I knew we had only a few precious hours in which to pack my belongings and leave.

One part of the plan that I could not think about was where I was going to live. One would think that would have been the first thing I thought about when leaving my husband. I am not sure why I didn't. It might have been faith, knowing that God would provide a place for me. But I probably did not have the ability to think about anything past moving day. I was so focused on every detail of the move and not getting caught that I rarely thought of anything else. So where I was to live was not high on my list. But one morning at work, I ran into Barb a friend of mine that I had not seen in several years. We had previously worked in the same department and she currently worked in a different department. We had remained in touch somewhat, but since marrying Joe, I had not talked with Barb.

When I saw Barb that morning, she suggested that we get together for lunch. I think she sensed I was not the same person she once knew. I was in the middle of planning to leave my husband, so I had a few things on my mind.

I agreed to meet for lunch. I had always had a great deal of respect for Barb. She asked me how things were going in my life. At that moment, I felt like I could trust Barb with anything. I described for her the abuse in my home and told her I was planning to leave. She asked me where I was going to live. I told her I did not have a clue. She simply stated that I was coming to live with her. We talked about it for a few more days and that was the end of my deciding where to live. I knew God sent Barb into my path that day. He made a way for me once again.

Everything seemed set for the move. I honestly do not think Joe noticed any change in me. God had allowed me to formulate my plan without Joe ever suspecting. I had the right amount of help and felt very good about the preparations I had made. God had given me peace in such a way that I did not have any doubts about everything going well. I did not even have a back up plan in case anything went wrong. Maybe that was wrong, but for me at the time, I had no doubts about what I was doing and I knew God was keeping me safe. I knew He had released me and I did not think He would have done that just for me to get caught in the last stage of the plan. I look back now and know it was just by God's grace that I was able to keep up my usual behaviors and demeanor with Joe. He never suspected anything was going on behind his back. I just had to make it through one more night and then I would be free from my captor of more than four years.

Chapter Ten: Perfection Execution

Commit to the Lord whatever you do,
and your plans will succeed.
Proverbs 16:3 (NIV)

My mind was racing the morning of my move. I slept very little the night before. I was not experiencing fear; I felt both excitement at being free and sadness that my marriage was ending the way that it was. I managed to go about my normal routine that morning and kissed Joe good-bye and told him I loved him, as I always did. I knew that would be the last time either of us said those words. They held no meaning, but I was feeling a loss. My emotions were going from hills to valleys and then back to hills.

My first stop was at the ATM machine to withdraw most of the little cash that was in our account. I took one hundred and forty dollars. That left twenty in the account. We had written a check for pizza the night before and I did not want it to bounce. How silly. But I took part of the money and filled my car with gas, went to McDonald's for breakfast, and then to a drug store to get a few small items.

After I had finished my errands, I drove to our prearranged meeting place and waited for the others to arrive. I knew Joe was going to the bank first thing that morning and he would drive past where we would be waiting. Penny was the first to arrive. She had asked if she could bring her niece with her. Penny did not want to make the drive by herself to help me move and she was not sure how she would be feeling on the drive home. Not only was it an important day for me, my best friend was so concerned and anxious for everything to go well for me. So when she and her niece arrived, I was very happy to see them. Then Jonathon arrived with all the boxes and Cathy pulled in right behind him. One other friend of mine, Roger, had known Joe and I from the beginning of our marriage. He now lived out of state with his wife Vicki and they both knew I was leaving that day. I had informed them via email of my plan to leave Joe. Without Joe knowing, Vicki and I had remained somewhat in touch after they moved out of state. Vicki had seen Joe lose his temper with me one time and I knew she and Roger would understand why I was leaving. So Roger had come into town to help with the move. I was so thankful. Then my parents arrived with the moving truck. I was not sure what kind of mood my mother was going to be in, but it did not take me long to find out. She got in my car while we were waiting and told me she guessed I did not need her help with all those other people there. I was not in a frame of mind to deal with anything from her so I simply told her then was not the time or place for that kind of talk. She still had to try and make everything about her. Her daughter was trying to get out of a horrible situation and she was concerned about whether or not she was needed. I am not sure if my mother truly wanted to help me move. I had actually not given her or my dad any choice about helping me. I had told them where I was in my life and what I needed from them. Right at that moment, I was not able to think about each individual and express my gratitude for everyone helping me. So she was not too happy about my comment, but I had more important issues on my mind right then.

Suddenly, my cell phone rang. From the caller ID, I saw it was work, so I answered it. I had just the day before told all the other people I worked with of my plan. I wanted them to be prepared for anything Joe might throw their way. I was not sure if he would go to my work when he realized I was gone, but I was certain he would call. So they were ready. And he indeed had called, asking for me. They told him I had gone downstairs for some breakfast and that I would return his call shortly. This usually satisfied him for about five minutes. They quickly phoned me that I needed to call him. I had told him that morning that I was to be in a meeting with my boss for an hour or so. Then we would go into our regular weekly meeting, which he always knew about. So I was supposed to be in the boss's office when he called. I returned his call at home, knowing our home phone did not have caller ID, and told him we were getting a late start on our meeting and that I had gone to get a muffin while I was waiting for my boss. He bought it. He just wanted to let me know that there had been a tornado in the area of Penny's house and that I might want to call her when I was through with the weekly meeting. I told him I would and then I was to call him. Joe never knew I was not at work. But I was able to ask Penny about the tornado and we both had a good chuckle at the thought that Joe did not know we were sitting next to each other in our cars on a parking lot less than one mile from him.

I had positioned my car so I would be able to see Joe drive by on his way to the bank, but he would not be able to see me. When I saw him go by, I sent Penny to follow him. She had always wanted to be a private detective so that assignment was right up her alley. But I had to be certain he went to the bank and then headed on to his job for the day and not back to the house from a different direction. Penny waited in a parking lot across from the bank and watched Joe. When he left the bank, she phoned me and told me the buzzard had left the bank. We were enjoying the comic relief of our silly jokes. She followed him as he drove past us, past the road to our house, and then he went on to the interstate. We waited five or ten minutes, knew he was not coming back for anything, and then rolled into action.

The first dilemma was how to get into the house. I could not get in through the front door because Joe locked it from the inside. But the key I had also fit the back door. There was a fence with a lock separating us from the back door. Of course I did not have a key to that lock. So I gave my backdoor key to Penny's niece, and the guys lifted her over the fence. She went in through the back door and let us in the front. I had tried to warn everyone about how filthy the house was. I tried not to be embarrassed, but I did not really care. I just wanted to pack and get out of there. Within two hours, everyone had packed everything on their lists; the boxes were labeled and loaded on the truck. I put my set of house keys, my cell phone, bankcards and any remaining checks I had, on the counter for Joe. I also left him a letter explaining very specifically why I had left. I did not want there to be any doubt in his mind about what he had done to me and that I would not be back. I was glad that we were able to finish in such a short time. But I still had to do one thing. I removed my socks and shoes and walked all over the couch in the living room and then I went into the bedroom and walked all over the bed, including Joe's pillow that I was sure he would sleep on that night. I cannot put into word how good it felt to do that. After having to deal with his feet issues for more than four years, it was almost therapeutic for me to walk with my shoes off. Everyone thought what I had done was such a good ending to the move. I had to agree.

We went outside and I borrowed Cathy's cell phone to page Joe. I told him I was on another phone because we had a gas leak at work and the building had been evacuated. As I look back now, I don't think I was very convincing. And I didn't care. I just wanted to buy the lab a little more time before they had to deal with Joe's anger. He had told me to call him back in one hour. I never did.

I left my prison for the last time and went to the post office to drop off a change of address card. Then everyone drove to my parents to unload my stuff and have lunch. I looked around at the people who had helped me and I realized there were seven people, the number of completion. I just smiled. I was glad God had given me just another confirmation of being completely free. I made a few phone calls to let some people know my mission had been accomplished and that I was safe. I called my work to let them know I was safe and they told me Joe had called. They simply said to him that they did not know where I was and that I had left. Joe asked them if I had left him. They did not know. I thought that was an interesting comment to make. Surely if one's wife were not at work, the last thought in your mind would be that she had left you. But on that day, Joe was right.

After we ate lunch, Cathy, who had left about thirty minutes earlier, suddenly reappeared at my parent's house. She said that Joe was calling everyone he knew to try and find me. But no one knew where I would be staying, not even Penny or my parents. I did not want anyone to have to lie or say anything that would allow him to find me, so I never told them. But his looking for me put me in a panic mode. I was not in fear of my life or anything like that, but not knowing how angry Joe was, I did not want him to come to my parent's and find me there. So I decided it was time for me to go to my new home. I was tired and ready to move on to the next phase of my life. I was excited and nervous all at the same time. But I knew God had led me down this path of freedom and He would continue on my journey with me as I started a new chapter in my life.

Part Three: Getting Healed

You intended to harm me,
but God intended it for good
to accomplish what is now being done.
Genesis 50:20 (NIV)

Chapter Eleven: Readjusting to Normal

But you must return to your God;
maintain love and justice,
and wait for your God always.
Hosea 12:6 (NIV)

As I drove to Barb's house, I tried to watch for people I knew on the road. I did not want anyone to know where I was going. I was definitely in a defensive frame of mind, especially after having experienced such an intensely emotional day. But I also had this overwhelming sense of hurting Joe. I was upset to think that I had caused another human pain. As I thought about this more, I realized that Joe was probably more upset about someone being in the house without him than he was about my having left. I also imagined that he was trying to figure how I had pulled off such a move without him ever knowing. He had tried to do such a good job of controlling my every move, but I had made the ultimate move without him. And I was sure he did not approve of my actions.

I arrived at my new home and Barb met me with a big hug. I just burst into tears. I realized my marriage was over. The one thing I had waited for, which should have been sacred and lasting, was over. Even though it had not even been close to being a healthy relationship, I still felt a loss. The whole move had been a success, but part of me felt like I had failed. But I had made the choice to leave and now I was in my new home. Barb helped me carry my few bags inside to my room. She had put fresh flowers in my room. What a warm welcome I received. At first, I did not feel comfortable putting things on the floor, since I had not been allowed to have anything touch the floor in more than four years. Barb tried to convince me that I could do anything I wanted and put anything anywhere I wanted, but I had a fear of doing the wrong thing or putting something in the wrong place. I spent a lot of time just crying that night. I did make a few phone calls to let people know I was out of my bondage. One person I spoke with had talked with Joe. She had asked Joe if everything I said about the way he had treated me was true and he said it was. I found it interesting that he did not deny what he had done to me. He had been caught with his hand in the cookie jar and was not denying the crime. But he did not understand why I had left. He could not comprehend that how he had treated me was wrong. And I did learn that he had a history of abuse. In that same phone conversation, he admitted that he had received two restraining orders in the past from other women. I had been advised by my pastor to have such an order placed against Joe, but that seemed so cruel. But after hearing of his history, I decided I would obtain a restraining order the next day.

I was at the end of my first day of freedom and I was exhausted. My emotions had gone the full spectrum from jubilation to devastation and then back. I never would have imagined that I would feel so many different emotions. I thought I would only feel joy and peace, which I did. But I also felt pain, sorrow, anger, and loss. I just wanted to go to bed. As I prepared to do just that, I realized I did not have any pajamas or proper sleeping attire. All the while I was married to Joe, I had to sleep in the nude, which I detested. The only time I had been able to sleep with some item of clothing on my body was when the furnace was broken and we were freezing. So I was not prepared to sleep like I wanted to that tonight. I managed to find a pair of shorts and a T-shirt that allowed me to feel comfortable enough to sleep. I just wanted to read my Bible, pray and go to sleep. I read the first sixty-eight chapters of Psalms that night. I was so hungry for the Word. I really had no one at that point to whom I felt I could turn and as I drew strength from what I read, I was ready for sleep.

I did not really sleep too well my first night of sleeping alone. There were too many new and different things around me for me to relax. But I woke to a very quiet house and I was able to read some more from the Bible. The words soothed my mind and reassured me that Someone knew where I was even when so many other people did not. I was ready to face my new day. I decided to unpack my clothes. That was more of a challenge than I ever could have imagined. Not only was I in a room all by myself, I was in a whole house by myself. Because of the rules I had allowed myself to live under, being in a house by myself was something that I had not done in more than four years! Now I had to make some decisions about things most people never gave a second thought. I had to put away my clothes. I had not been allowed to do any laundry or take responsibility for hanging up my clothes. Joe was under the impression that either I was not able to do it for myself, I would do it wrong, or let something fall on the floor while I was doing it. But that first day at Barb's, I actually placed and hung my clothes the way I wanted without anyone telling me how to do it, doing it for me, or yelling at me for doing it wrong. I did not have a lot to put away, but I would place something and then catch myself worrying if that were the correct way or not. Besides, I had to make sure none of the items ever touched the floor. If that had happened when I was with Joe, the items were thrown away. But as I placed each item, the unpacking became easier.

Next I had to focus all my attention on an area where the most rules had applied when I was with Joe. I was faced with the big challenge of unpacking my shoes. I had been conditioned that anything to do with feet was filthy. Every time I had put on or taken off shoes and socks over the past four years, I had washed my hands. Now I was faced with a whole bag of shoes and no one was watching me. I really had to fight the fear of not washing my hands after touching them. What if someone knew I had touched them and then not washed? I had experienced the wrath of not washing and I did not want to ever feel that wrath again. I finally managed to finish putting all of my clothes and shoes away. It was a great mental hurdle I crossed over and I sat back and admired what I had accomplished. I felt like I had built a mansion for a king. I was very proud of myself. I was exhausted, but felt fulfilled.

I took a peaceful shower and dressed how I wanted for my day. I constantly found myself looking out for things touching the floor or not touching my feet. I still had not realized how much my mind had been programmed to think like Joe wanted me to think. I had spent so much time with him and had been so controlled by him, that in some ways, my thinking began to be like his. I had begun to lose my identity when I was with Joe and I did not want that to continue. I needed to be as far from him as possible to be able to find myself again. And I needed to know he could not come near me. With that thought, I was about to give myself some peace of mind as I headed to the courthouse to apply for a restraining order. I was totally lost in trying to do such things. That was something I thought I would never know how to do. But for my peace of mind, I went. The judge eventually issued the order for one year. I felt better knowing Joe could not try to contact me or even come close to me for that length of time.

After receiving the restraining order, I needed to stop by a store and purchase a few things. I went into K-Mart and started looking at pajamas. All of a sudden, I felt like I had never felt before in my life. My heart started racing and I was breaking out in a sweat. I thought I was being watched and that I was not supposed to be there. I felt like I was going to get caught and then get in trouble for being somewhere I was not supposed to be. I started moving very quickly to the door and rushed out to my car. I just sat there and cried. I did not know what to do or why I was feeling like I felt. But it made me upset that I had not been able to get pajamas. So I had a little pep talk with myself, prayed for God to calm my emotions, and marched back into the store. I was moving fast, but I managed to grab the first pair of pj's in my size, some cereal, and an empty journal book. If anyone had been with me, they would have thought the store was on fire because of how fast I was moving. But I was determined to make a purchase.

As I walked to the front toward the checkout, I saw some cute summer shirts on sale. I did not have a lot of money at that point, but they were so bright and cheery. So I quickly found my size and then paid for my items. I felt like I had broken one of the Ten Commandments in buying that shirt. I sat in the car for a few minutes and told myself I was totally nuts for being upset and that I had every right to buy myself a shirt, especially at $4.99! I was feeling like the money should have been put toward a bill and I was also nervous about whether Joe would approve of my purchase. I had not bought any of my own clothes for more than four years. As I sat in the car arguing with myself, I became very nervous that someone who knew Joe might see me and tell him, so I hurriedly left and went home.

All in all, my first day of freedom had been good. I was glad to have had time to reflect and let my emotions come and go. I intentionally had not given my new phone number to people. I did not want to have people calling me all the time to see how I was doing. If I needed someone, I called them. That gave me time with myself and with God and I needed both of those. I was not in any position to handle too much pressure and I did not want to hear fifty voices telling me what I should or should not do. I knew that everyone had my best interest at heart, but I needed to hear from God. I still at that time did not realize the depth of help I needed from God. I unknowingly was laying an important foundation in turning to Him and learning to look to Him for my answers. He was tucking me away from influences other than His and I did not even know it. So once again, He was making a way for me. And I needed Him for the things I was to face over the next few weeks and months.

Chapter Twelve: Aftershocks

*Restore to me the joy of your salvation
and grant me a willing spirit, to sustain me.
Psalm 51:12 (NIV)*

As I began a new day, I read from the Bible to let the words wash over me and soak into me. I only wanted to read Psalms because it covers all the emotions. After I had finished reading, I decided to make another run at being in public. I thought perhaps if I went to a smaller store, I would not feel as panicked as I had in K-Mart. I stopped at a convenience store and picked up a few items. Again, I felt like I was being watched and that I was going to get in some kind of trouble for being there without Joe. I found myself moving very quickly and not wanting to be seen. But I did manage to make my purchases, which I perceived as a huge accomplishment.

After all my purchasing, I had worked up an appetite and decided to get a bite to eat. I thought about all the times I had eaten with Joe and how traumatic it was with him making a decision where to eat. He had always told me to pick a restaurant, but he never liked what I picked, didn't want that type of food, the restaurant would be too crowded, or he didn't like where we were seated. So I never really picked and now that I had my chance, I could not make a decision. I drove around for almost an hour without being able to find a place I thought would be enjoyable. I think I really did not feel comfortable making a decision knowing that Joe would not approve. I finally came home in tears and asked God to renew my ability to make decisions.

The next few days continued to bring waves of emotions to me. I did not attend church the first week after leaving Joe. Someone had talked with Joe and knew he was going to be there, so I decided not to go. I was not sure if I was mentally prepared to see him or to be around so many people at once. I was actually fearful of seeing him. I was still in a bit of a state of shock. I knew I would be able to pray and spend time with God on His day. But as that Sunday passed, I grew angry with myself for not attending church. I realized that my not going was still allowing Joe to control me. I had not been able to see that at first, but when I did, I was very angry. He had controlled me for more than four years, I had left him, and he was still controlling me. At that time I made the firm decision to be at church the following Sunday, Joe or no Joe!

Seeing that I had left Joe, I needed to begin the process of permanently severing all ties with him. Someone had asked me if I would consider giving Joe a chance to go to therapy and then return to him. I thought about that for a day or two and decided that if Joe did go for help, he needed to do that for himself. He could not get help just to get me back. It would have to be something he did on his own for himself. That would be the only way it would mean anything to him. And I honestly could not imagine returning to any kind of life with Joe. I had made my decision to leave him completely, no matter how much I hated that my marriage was over. I was going to start down a road of unfamiliar territory and I was not happy about traveling that road. I hated the thought of going to a lawyer's office. That was another one of those things I thought I would never have to know anything about. I did not realize the things I would learn over the next few months that I never wanted to know. I did not want to know how to obtain a restraining order, but I had. I had never wanted to know how to file for a divorce, but I was learning. I never wanted to see my life broken down as a statistic, but that was happening. So many issues that I knew nothing about were now being thrown my way at a rapid pace. I did not even begin to know how to find a lawyer. I prayed for God to direct me. I had asked the center for abused women for some names and I called one of the females on the list. At this point, I did not want to deal with any males! I made an appointment, filled out some paper work and paid a large sum of money. I was shocked at how much it costs to end a marriage. But knowing I was going to be free from Joe was worth every penny. I did not care how much it cost. I had committed to paying my tithes first and I knew God would take care of all the rest.

My emotions were still on their daily roller coaster ride. I would wake up, spend time with the Lord each day, and try to find some sort of normalcy in my day. I went to work and tried to make myself leave my desk at the times I knew Joe used to always call. I made a conscious effort to try and do things that were different from the routine of when I was married to him. I wanted to break the trap of control that had its grip on my mind. At times I did feel sorry for the pain I thought I was causing Joe. I had tried so hard while I was married to Joe to always do things to please him. I knew how he felt when he was not pleased with me, which in turn caused me pain. If he did not feel pain, neither did I. So in my mind, I thought since I was in so much pain, he surely must be feeling pain also. It was a cause and effect that had been instilled in my brain over the past four years. I was still trying to not cause Joe any pain. Then I would get upset with myself for feeling that way. I tried to make myself see that I was not responsible for Joe's feelings and any pain he was feeling because of my actions, he would just have to deal with. I tried not to feel guilty, but my emotions were unstable and the guilt came easy, which made me upset with Joe and myself. I then felt guilty for feeling upset and cried a lot. But as I cried, I prayed that God would restore my emotions to a steady state so I could get on with my life.

I knew I was going to see Joe the next Sunday at church and I tried to prepare myself for that. One thing I knew I must do was purchase a new outfit. I was very nervous about shopping for a Sunday outfit without Joe. But I made myself go to a department store and shop. I did not have the panic attacks like I had previously. I thanked God for that. I managed to pick out an outfit that I liked and tried very hard to not think about whether or not Joe would like it. I wanted to look very nice on Sunday. I did not want to look like I was depressed or upset or even sad. I wanted to continue to put on my smiling face like nothing was wrong.

So when Sunday came, I put on my new outfit and my best smile as I headed to church. Barb told me I was looking very sharp before I left the house. It was so good to have her encouraging me. I was very nervous, but determined to get there. I saw Cathy first and she gave me a big hug. Everyone loved my new outfit. As I was visiting with people in the foyer, I peeked into the sanctuary and saw Joe. He did not see me or at least he was not looking my way. I just cried. Cathy was there to help me maintain my composure. I had thought I would not cry, but I did. I found my seat with Cathy and her friend Fern. We had a guest speaker that service and he actually talked about how men should treat women. I wept through the whole service. I just prayed that God would see me through the service and give me the strength to walk out the door to go home.

When it came time to leave, Cathy and Fern walked with me to my car. They each walked on either side of me. I felt like I had my own personal bodyguards. They did not let anyone get to me that I did not want to see. Little did I know that I was walking with two prayer warriors who would soon become my armor bearers. I did not know at the time, but they would be there for me, praying for me, protecting me, and helping me in any way they could. But most importantly, they would walk with me down the path of spiritual and emotional healing I was about to begin. God was starting to set me up to travel down a new road and He knew the strength it would take for me to travel that road. The only preparation I had for my journey was I knew He would never give me more than I could bear and He had already traveled the road before me and would be waiting for me at the end. I would have to cling to those promises many times over the next part of my journey.

Chapter Thirteen: Slowly Healing

Create in my a pure heart, O God,
and renew a stead-fast spirit within me.
Psalm 51:10 (NIV)

As the months passed by, I grew stronger every day. Barb allowed me to feel any emotion and never told me to get over it or that it was time to move on. God had placed me in a safe place with her and I was very grateful for her patience with me and my healing process. She was the best entertainment for me. She was always doing something silly or crazy to make life interesting. She shot me with water pistols and taught me new games to play. She even provided entertainment by making a cream cheese dip in a bowl the dog had eaten out of. She did not realize what she had done and she ate a lot of the dip. When she found out what had happened, she was sick, but it was so funny. I never knew what was going to happen next with Barb and I enjoyed that.

I went to a counselor my pastor had recommended and the counselor reassured me I was on the right path to returning to a normal life. He was amazed at how well I was coping considering all I had been through with Joe. I credited my healing to my faith and dependence on God. Joe was also seeing the same counselor at a different location and different time. That was when I learned Joe was diagnosed with some mental disorders, which explained a lot of things to me. Whether or not he continued to seek help, I don't know. He no longer attended church and I did not see him until well over a year after the divorce was final. I had not talked with him since the day I left. I went through the divorce process and experienced many sad emotions from the ordeal. To see something I had dreamed of ending in black and white was very difficult for me to handle. I hated being put in the situation of divorce. I felt my heart had been broken by someone that I wanted to love, trust, and spend the rest of my life with.

I never wanted to divorce. Joe was to be my one and only and that was how he had presented himself before we were married. I cried many days until I could not cry anymore. Many days I felt numb. I would not say the divorce was easy, no matter how desperately I wanted to be free from Joe. But God was with me through all of it and I prayed daily for Him to guide and protect me through the process. My lawyer turned out to be perfect for me and always looked out for my best interest. I ended up receiving money back that I had paid her and Joe had to pay all court costs and other fees. I knew that was from God. Joe had to sell some of his prized possessions and give me a portion of the proceeds. I had grown past the point of feeling sad for him or thinking I was hurting him in some way. I only felt sorry for him that he was so unhappy and did not even realize it.

I needed to know I was an individual again, able to make decisions on my own and lead a normal life. I grew better at making routine decisions such as where to eat or what to buy in a store. I prayed so much during that time because I knew He was always there, even when I felt no one else understood. I tried not to feel sorry for myself, or if I did, only for a few minutes. I knew the road of self-pity would only leave me bitter and empty. I continued to go to church regularly and everyone said I looked radiant. I was feeling free from the control that had been placed on my life by Joe. I was relearning the art of conversation. So many of my emotions had been shut down while I was with Joe and I found myself having a difficult time talking with people. I felt as if what I had to say was of so little importance. Joe had never really cared what I had to say and I had grown to think everyone else thought the same way about me. I talked with Penny, Barb, Cathy, and Fern as much as I felt I could. I often had a hard time sharing issues because of feeling inadequate or insignificant.

My church offered a divorce recovery class just as I was going through my divorce. Once again, God was on time. They had not offered the class in quite a few years, but I felt it was for me so I accepted the challenge. It made me feel normal to hear other people were having the same emotions. Through the class, I discovered that I was still very angry with Joe. While I was married, it had not been in my best interest to show my anger at something he did or said. So I had stored all the anger from four years inside. I already had a problem managing anger, since I had made the decision as a child to not have a temper. I had all these feeling of anger in me, but did not have a healthy way of dealing with them. Someone in the class suggested writing a letter to the person with whom I was angry. I spent some time writing Joe and telling him exactly how I felt about what he had done to me. I think the exercise of writing my feelings was very therapeutic. Up to this point, I was totally blaming Joe for how he treated me. I did not yet see that I had allowed him to control and abuse me. But my eyes were soon to be opened.

As I was taking the divorce recovery class, another class was being offered entitled Caring for People God's Way. [2] It was a class designed to train people to be lay counselors within the church. I was in no way interested in becoming a lay counselor. I was just finishing counseling myself and trying to get my life refocused to where God wanted me to go and I knew it was not counseling. But I could not get the class out of my mind. Everywhere I turned, someone was talking about it and telling me I should take the class. I just did not want to do it, but as the deadline for registration drew closer, I felt in the pit of my stomach that I better take that class. I was almost to the point of feeling sick if I did not enroll. So on the last possible date, I paid my fee and completed the registration form. As soon as I had made the commitment, I felt peace in my spirit and the feeling in the pit of my stomach left. I was not sure what was going on, but I guessed God was trying to tell me something and I finally got it. I told almost no one that I was taking the class. I did not tell even Barb or Penny. I was afraid people would think I was on a mission to save the whole world since I had just survived a divorce and been through counseling. But I certainly did not have all the answers and I was not even looking for them.

When the class started, I was just going through the motions. I took notes and was learning new ideas and concepts, but to be honest, I was bored. The instructor was very knowledgeable on the topics, but I did not feel challenged. I talked with Fern about the class. She had taken the class the previous year and just thought it was wonderful. I felt like I had missed the mark because I was not getting anything out of it. She encouraged me to hang in there with the class and let God show me what I needed to see. I was continuing to pray that God would show me areas where I needed change. Our pastor had recently preached a sermon where he talked about worshiping God with clean hands and a pure heart. He stated that we really worshiped with all that was within us. His words struck a nerve with me. I was certain there was junk inside of me that was not pleasing to Him and I was trying to worship Him through all the junk. So my daily prayer became for Him to show me areas that I needed to clean up. I had often heard people say, be careful what you pray for, you just might get it. I know now that is a true statement. I was about to find out I wished I had never prayed that prayer.

Chapter Fourteen: Baggage Exposed

So I turned my mind to understand,
to investigate and to search out wisdom and the scheme of things
and to understand the stupidity of wickedness and the
madness of folly.
Ecclesiastes 7:25 (NIV)

I was continuing to heal and establish some normal routines in my life. I felt I had completely severed my ties with Joe. The divorce was finalized and I felt free from him and what he had done to me. But I was struggling to find my place in society. I had gone from single to married to divorced. In each previous stage, I had always been able to find my place or purpose. Now I was feeling isolated and not a part of anything. I was not connected with any groups at church where social events were organized. Such groups existed, I just never felt like I wanted to take part. I was still very insecure in whom I was but did not see it. I was wrestling with joining the choir at church, and finally did, but I felt very insecure about being there. I was not sure where God wanted me to be, but I knew I would have to be somewhere. I had never been a pew warmer and being divorced should not change that for me. I tried to consistently be in the Word and in prayer about what direction I needed to take. I knew if I kept God first and foremost in my life, He would direct me.

I was still trying to find some meaning in my taking the lay counseling class. We had covered such topics as helping others find significance in life, overcoming depression, and understanding the power of truth. Part of me felt like I was just wasting my time with the class. The information was good, but

I knew I was never going to use any of what I was learning. But I had paid money and made a commitment, so I continued. The sixth lesson was entitled "Surviving sexual abuse: On the Threshold of Hope." [3] I read the title before the class began and thought to myself again there would be nothing for me in the lesson. I had been abused, dealt with it and the issue was closed. As the class proceeded, the information showed how abuse as a child often affects people in their adult lives. The text stated some of the aftereffects of childhood sexual abuse that an adult could have. Children who had been abused often grow up hating their bodies and can develop eating disorders or problems with food or sex. Abused people also often suffer from emotional problems such as anger, guilt, fear, or just shut down their emotions all together. They think they are worthless and do not trust and think others are going to betray them or reject them. It is also hard for victims to believe God loves them or cares about them. I heard all of those things and thought I had experienced a few of them, but I was over any damage that had been done to me because of abuse. It had taken place so many years ago and I thought I had healed. So I still felt like there was nothing for me in that lesson.

We had a substitute instructor that evening, Sue, who made the statement that many people who marry abusive partners were often sexually abused when they were children. As soon as those words left her mouth, my emotions went into something that could only be described as complete chaos. I was immediately transported back many years to old issues I had buried. I felt angry, hurt, confused, disappointed, rejected, and totally isolated all at the same time. I did not hear another word from the class and just wanted to get out of there and go home where I felt safe. I totally shut everything and everybody out for the next few days. I was in a lot of pain and did not know why. I could not pray or read my Bible. I did not feel like eating, crying, talking, or singing. I just wanted to be left alone. Barb was concerned and I just told her I was going through something and I would be all right, but I certainly did not feel all right. I managed to suppress some emotions without really dealing with any of my issues until the next week when we returned to class. I just wanted to move on to the next topic.

Our regular instructor, Mary Jo, had returned and I was certain she would jump right into our next lesson. But instead, Mary Jo discussed sexual abuse again and related some of the same information Sue had given the previous week. My emotions began to rage as they had in the last lesson. I did not know how to handle the anger I was feeling. I was mad at the world and did not care about anything. Cathy and Fern were very concerned and told me if I needed to talk, they were there for me. I could not talk with anyone because I really did not understand all the negative emotions I was experiencing. I was thinking the abuse was my fault and I must have done something bad to deserve it. I knew I was not worthy of anything from anybody because of what had happened to me. I was not worthy to love or be loved. I felt so ashamed. I continued to shut everyone out. I did not want to deal with any of the stuff that was going through my head. I just wanted to press it down to where it had been for so many years and have it not raise its ugly head again.

But God was not going to let me get off the hook so easy. He was trying to get my attention and continued to knock at my door. The very next week, a special seminar at church had been scheduled and Mary Jo had requested for our counseling class to attend. I was not in any frame of mind to be attending a seminar, but I had said I would be there and I kept my word. Cathy and Fern were also attending, so I thought if they were there, it might not be all that bad. When I heard the topic of the seminar, I wished I had not gone. Trauma and traumatic events such as sexual, verbal, and physical abuse were going to be discussed. I was not excited when I heard the topics and the confusion and anger continued to churn within me. I had been hoping for something on love, joy and peace. That was what I thought I needed, but God had other plans. I managed to endure the session, but was still very angry inside. I was having to think about the abuse I had suffered as a child. I had to look at how the sexual abuse had affected my way of thinking, how I viewed myself and how I felt other people viewed me.

There was a prayer at the close of the seminar and I just sat there for a few minutes. Fern was sitting beside me and Cathy behind me. I was surrounded by my armor bearers. I knew I had to say something to them. I was in a tremendous amount of pain and had never been so confused in all my life. I had no idea why I was feeling like I was and did not know what to do with all my out of control emotions. I had shared many stories with them regarding my situation with Joe and they had always supported me, prayed for me and pointed me to God. I was just afraid they would tell me the abuse was my fault, or that I was overreacting and it hadn't really been all that bad. Or they might even think I was making everything up. The only other person I had ever told had been Joe and he used my secret against me. Now I was on the verge of telling two more people and I did not know what their reactions were going to be, but I knew I had to let them know I was struggling.

Telling Fern and Cathy that I had been sexually abused was one of the hardest things I had ever done in my life. I did not go into a lot of details. I was in too much pain and just saying the words was an effort. They were very compassionate and supportive. They prayed with me and I appreciated their concern and prayers. I felt a little better, but I was still very confused. I did not have the peace I was hoping to feel and wondered if God truly loved me. Perhaps He was angry with me for having never dealt with my stuff. I felt like I was being punished.

As I continued to feel hurt and confusion, I still was not able to pray about any of my feelings. Perhaps I felt too embarrassed or was afraid God would not hear my prayer. I just knew I could not reach Him. I usually enjoyed singing in my car, but I had not been able to even offer singing as a sacrifice. I had listened to a song entitled Waymaker [4] over and over. I heard nothing else for more than a week. That song became my prayer. I needed to have a way made for me because I did not know how to make one for myself. The next Sunday, I went searching for Him. I needed to connect with Him and know that He was still there for me. I did not know if I was going to hear from God that day or not, but the choir started singing Waymaker. I could not believe it. I knew God was somehow going to make a way for me. I found a place in the corner and just started pouring my heart out to Him. I knew He was the only one who had been with me through all my hurts and He saw the turmoil that was in my soul. Surely He could meet me where I was. Cathy and Fern were immediately at my side, pouring prayers over me. I continued to weep before the Lord and begged Him to help me. I so desperately wanted to be like Him and free from my pain.

When I finished crying and seeking God's face, I felt as if I had lost a hundred pounds. My armor-bearers prayed over me again, hugged me, and told me they loved me. Many people had told me they loved me my whole life and I knew they did, but I never felt loved. But that day, I think I truly felt like somebody loved me for the first time in my life. I honestly believed Fern and Cathy when they spoke those words to me. But more important, I knew I was a different person. I did not feel the shame I had carried for years. I had asked God to take it from me and He had honored my request. I went home and looked at myself in a mirror. I saw a different person. I could actually look at myself in the mirror and like what I saw. But I also felt God liked what He saw. I was not ready to share my secret with the whole world, but I felt I needed to tell Barb. She had been so concerned about me and I wanted to reassure her I was doing better. So I shared with Barb about my having been sexually abused. It was much easier to say the second time. She hugged me and told me she loved me. She was very supportive and thanked me for trusting her enough to share with her one of my deepest secrets.

I knew I had obtained a small victory that Sunday morning, but I still had some issues to address. At least I knew God was with me and He was listening to me and answering my cries for help. I had hope in places where I thought hope would never be. The things that had been in darkness were now ready to be brought out into the light.

Chapter Fifteen: More Light Than Darkness

Then your light shall break forth like the morning,
your healing shall spring forth speedily,
and your righteousness shall go before you.
The glory of the Lord shall be your rear guard.
Then you shall call, and the Lord will answer;
you shall cry, and He will say, here I am.
Isaiah 58:8-9 (NIV)

I was slowly able to think more about the decisions I had made as a child. As I did so, I began to see how they had affected many areas of my life. I had always felt like I needed the approval of certain individuals and worked very hard to try and win that approval. This was particularly true with my mother. I can truthfully say that now, I do not have any anger toward my mother and I do not hold any unforgiveness toward her. I understand why my dad is passive, even though I may not agree with how he handled things. I do not think being passive is the way to deal with difficult situations and I wish I had not learned to be like him. I love both my parents and am thankful they are still in my life today. But I know I allowed my parents to impact my life in a very dramatic way. I tried to do everything perfect just to be able to please them. I did what I could to please every adult in my life, thinking they would tell my parents how good I had been. I always received the top grade in my classes at school. I worked hard around our yard, keeping it nice and well groomed. I tried my best to be quiet as a mouse in the mornings getting ready for school while my mother slept. I did not talk back to my parents and never caused them any headaches. I would do almost anything any adult asked me to do, hoping it would please my parents. I became a people pleaser and did not realize it. But to me it seemed I was never able to do things just quite well enough to please my mother. So, growing up, I often felt inadequate and frustrated. And now that I was trying to look at all areas of my life, I realized how many different feelings I had toward my mother.

I was not comfortable with how she treated me either as a child or as an adult. She never called me and I felt like she never tried to form a relationship with me, but I thought it was my fault that we did not have a mother-daughter bond. She would often have my sister inform me of a family function instead of personally telling me. What had I done that was so bad that made me feel like my mother did not like me? I felt unloved by her and did not understand why. When we were together, my part of the conversation was always strained. I was afraid that anything I said was going to be taken the wrong way or blown out of proportion. I was very guarded with my words. I was afraid to speak my mind for fear of hearing disapproval of what I had to say. I felt my opinion did not matter and I learned to live in fear. But while all the confusing feelings were flowing through me, I also desperately wanted her approval. I would try to find the right words to say and do almost anything to please her. As matter of fact, it seemed most of the family went along with whatever she said just to avoid arguments. I learned that most issues were not worth arguing about. I became very complacent. I had indeed become my dad.

So I had all these thoughts racing through my head and could not put them in any order that made sense to me. I felt like another dark cloud was over me and I could not think clearly enough to move it. I began to shut people out and turned inward, hoping to get control of my emotions. I prayed that God would help me understand my feelings toward my mother and rid me of the guilt I was feeling. I felt so much guilt for years about not having a relationship with my mother and then, as an adult, extra guilt for not wanting a relationship with her. I needed balance but could not find it. I was going through the motions of living and trying to handle a heavy burden at the same time. My countenance was growing more somber each day as I tried to find my way out of the darkness that was enclosing around me. People who were close to me knew I was troubled by something. But I was still trying to figure out my own thoughts and feelings and did not have the words to say what was in me.

Once again, Cathy and Fern were watching me and trying to see if they could intervene. They were so good to never push me to talk about anything. They just quietly waited and prayed. Finally, I could not stand the pressure in my head anymore. I felt I was the worst person on the face of the earth for what I was thinking and I had to get it out. My armor bearers already knew more about me than anyone else, so I had to continue to trust them. I finally broke down and shared with them that I did not understand my mother and I did not think I wanted an intimate relationship with her. My statement may not have seemed like a big issue to them, but at that time, it was my world. I felt such guilt. They both listened as I shared my feelings and then pointed me to the Word. God reached into my life when I was merely a tiny embryo and began to shape me within, He formed me. He began to put me together while I was still in the soft silence of my mother's womb. It was there You created my inmost being. (Psalm 139:13 NIV) They showed me it was God who made me, not my parents. He was the one that was to care for me. And Fern pointed out that my mother probably did not care about me. I remember looking at her with a face of shock. I had not expected to hear such a bold statement and they were not the easiest words to hear. But she continued with her explanation and told me my mother probably did not know HOW to care about me. She was probably wounded herself and was incapable of loving me, as I needed to be loved. Cathy said to me later that people who feel unloved couldn't work through their own issues enough to love themselves or others. So they will often create situations to make everyone else as miserable as they are, then they think they win! I may never know what my mother's wounds were, but I no longer have to strive to have an intimate relationship with her. But I do love her because God loves her and I do honor her because she is my mother. I did feel a sense of loss when I came to the realization that there was something in my life that I always wanted, but had never had. And for that I truly did grieve.

As time passed, my eyes continued to be opened to the truth about my mother, Joe and myself. I saw that in reality, when I married Joe, I married my mother. I had been so comfortable living in fear of my mother, that I somehow attracted someone else that I could fear. Fear of disappointing and fear of rejection had become my comfort zones and I thought I was happy there. I was very good at learning the rules and doing whatever I could to please others and keep peace. But the Bible says Blessed are the Peacemakers (Matthew 5:9, NIV). It says nothing about the peacekeepers. I had to learn who I was and be comfortable with how God made me. I was eventually able to see that I was not responsible for how other people felt toward me or how they treated me. I am only responsible for my actions and my words. Now I truly feel love toward my mother. But it is His love through me that allows me to love her. I no longer view her as responsible for the abuses I suffered as a child. And I no longer hold her responsible for my living in fear of people for all those years. I must depend on God to guide me and listen for His voice to direct me. Every day was a new journey with Him and I continued to press into Him.

Chapter Sixteen: Taking Out the Trash

I will cleanse you of your filthy behavior.
Ezekiel 36:29 (NIV).

Over several months, I had been able to look at my life from a new perspective. I was becoming happy with myself and who I was in Christ. He had allowed me to have many hurts in my life so I could finally see myself the way He saw me. I was continually trying to please Him and seek His will for my life. I had closed the door on many of my past hurts and was truly experiencing some of the joy of the Lord.

But there was still one area of my life where I had not been able to experience victory and that was in the area of the addiction in my life. I had not seen how much I depended on that force. It had become such a steady part of my life, I never thought about it as all that bad. I was using it to fill a void. I occasionally felt a small amount of guilt and remorse, but not enough to keep me from returning to it. But I was wounded and my habit allowed me to feel some sort of love. I was still reaching out in the only way my crippled mind knew to find love. When I was a child, I had translated the sexual abuse into love. The person who had abused me was gentle and spoke softly to me and I had interpreted that abuse as love. So the addiction in my life took me back to a time when I thought I felt love. It was a sick way to receive love, but as a child who thought about that attention as love, I desperately wanted to hold on to that feeling of love. I had kept the habit in my life for years and was very comfortable with it. It had been with me when I was lonely, and when I felt no one loved me. The addiction would only come alive when I was by myself and often after I had spent time with my family. I always came away from my family feeling so empty and needing a fix. At one time, I thought I had been relieved of my crutch, but it returned and I was more dependent on it than ever before. But as I drew closer to God, I felt more guilt regarding that area of my life. I was still praying for God to show me anything in my life that was not pleasing to Him. And once again He did not fail to answer my prayer.

He continued to speak to me through the Caring for People God's Way class. I was beginning to see why I had to take that class. God knew I would pay attention to Mary Jo because my whole life, I never wanted to disappoint an authority figure. So I listened when we were on the lesson that dealt with the area of addictions. I was hearing how I had felt for years, but had never been able to express. It was at that time that I realized I needed God to help me get rid of my crutch. Never before had I seen my dependence for what it was and now I understood why I had kept it active in my life for so long. But I did not want people to find out I had such an evil presence in my life. I was a faithful choir member, regular tither, involved with the benevolence ministry and part of the altar courtesy team. How could I have such an evil presence on me and more important, how could I tell anyone I had this in my life?

For one month after having had the lesson on addictions, I struggled immensely with how to overcome the sin in my life. I knew the sin would not keep me from going to heaven, but I knew it was keeping me from a closer relationship with God. During that month, the more I tried to deny its presence, the stronger it grew. And I felt there was no one with whom I could share my pain. I could never tell Cathy and Fern about my problem. The thought of them knowing about it sickened me. I was sure they would not understand and I honestly was too embarrassed to tell them. So I felt completely alone in the battle, which led to my leaning on my crutch more and more. I finally came to the point of total despair. I was at the lowest point ever in my life and I had no one to whom I could turn. God had led me to a point where I could only turn to Him. He had proven himself over and over to me and I knew He was the only source of help. I fell on my face before Him one evening at home and just wept uncontrollably. I was more broken than I had ever been in my life. I admitted I had a problem and could not solve it without His help. In fact I begged Him to take my crutch from me. I was at the end of the road. I had a battle I did not know how to fight and obviously was not strong enough to fight it. I needed Him to come along side and deliver me. I tried to read the Word for some answers, but none of what I read was getting inside me. I had all the embarrassment and pain from the evil surrounding me and it seemed nothing could penetrate that wall. I once again needed to hear from God. I had learned that if I could only get to Jesus, He would make a way. I simply prayed that He would speak to me and relieve me of my torment.

I went to church the following Sunday and discovered we were having a guest speaker. I was not thrilled with that idea. I had been able to hear from God through my pastor in the past and I was not sure I could hear from Him through someone else. But when God wants to get a word to us and we are listening, He will use any available vessel. She was the founder/director of a center in Pennsylvania whose focus was to restore broken lives. She talked about how God wanted to change our lives forever.

She called on the congregation to consecrate itself that day, for tomorrow the Lord was going to do great things in each of our lives. I could not help but think that He could not do anything in my life with all the sin I had in me. But she said God was able to dismiss things from our lives and we had to let them go. We simply had to call on Him and He would deliver us. I took that very personally. I had been calling on Him to take my addiction from me, but I did not know if He had heard me. Then she began to read my mail. She said often we want to stop things, but we can't. I understood that statement all too well. But she encouraged me when she said God was going to deliver me and that the thing that had been holding me back was not going to take me out. God was the only one who could deliver me. She simply stated there were people there that day who were so bound and did not want anyone to know anything about their sin. She even said that some people had been tormented by issues for years. Again, those statements hit home with me. My prop was something I never wanted anyone to know about and it was also something I could not get rid of on my own. So I was stuck and in need of help from God. And then she stated that when we come to God, it is really no one's business but God's and it is His delight to bless us and set us free.

I felt confident that I had heard from God and that He would honor my request to remove my sin from my life. I found a place to pray and again poured my heart out to Him and simply asked Him to remove my sin and replace it with whatever He had for me. I felt like God heard my cry and met me where I was that day. I felt His presence in a powerful way and I knew beyond anything that He had freed me from the evil presence. I felt a sense of peace like I have never felt before. When God brought me to a place of true repentance, I was broken before Him and I was never to return to my crutch. I told the speaker that day I knew God had delivered me. She told me I had to tell someone what God had done, but I did not have to give any specifics. I found Fern after the service and told her what I had just experienced. I had mentioned to her at one time I had an issue in my life that I had dealt with for years. When I mentioned it to Fern the first time, I was trying to give it up on my own. I was not successful. I told her that what I thought had left me before had returned. But the second time, God had taken it from me. I knew in my heart of hearts that I was never to be tormented by that part of my past again.

God had gone to the root of the problem and pulled it out from there. I had called upon His name and He had answered me. I had trusted Him and He had not failed. Where the pain had been, He placed His love and I felt it.

Chapter Seventeen: New Joy

Forget the former things, do not dwell on the past.
See I am doing a new thing!
Now it springs up; do you not perceive it?
Isaiah 43: 18-19 (NIV).

I am not able to put into words the joy I felt at having been set free of my addiction. I could say I was experiencing joy unspeakable. I knew beyond a shadow of a doubt that I would never deal with that disgusting sin again. I went home after that powerful service and just fell on my face and worshiped God. I wept tears of joy and thanksgiving before Him and thanked Him for once again making a way for me when I could not find the way. Since that day, I have not even been tempted to return to my old ways. I can honestly say I have been in situations that in the past would have been very difficult for me to handle without leaning on something superficial. But in each of those situations, I have felt like a different person, I have had a different outlook, and I have handled them differently than I would have in the past. I have learned who I am in God and how very much He loves me. I have rejoiced that He has always been there for me. I no longer need a fix to make it through a difficult time. I rarely think about what had been in my life, only to rejoice in the fact that it is no longer a part of me. I do remember the date of having been set free and praise God on the anniversary. I know what it was like to have been bound and then freed. And I know what it is like to have God do something in me where I will never be the same again.

After God fought the battle for my deliverance, I had such a sweet peace in my soul. I knew all the major problems that were attached to my mother, being sexually abused, physically and emotionally abused, and dealing with an evil addiction, were past. I know my enemy well and he can never bring those issues up to me again. The enemy somehow gets stuff in us, but it is God who gets it out. There was nothing I did to provide for my healing or deliverance. God provided everything. I was just willing and seeking Him. The Word asks, Is there anything too hard for God? (Genesis 18:14 NIV) I know I was able to wake each morning with a song in my heart for the day. I was able to see God in ways I never had before. When I was younger, I had wished that my mother would hug me or hold me, but I did not receive nurturing from her. Can a woman forget her nursing child, and not have compassion on the son of her womb? Surely they may forget, but I will not forget you. (Isaiah 49:15 NIV) So I had asked Him to just wrap His arms around me and hold me. Oftentimes I did not feel His love. But now I can see He was always loving me through other people. It may not have been the people I wanted it from, but He had placed very special people in my life to love me and help me grow. I am thankful today for those people and I am able to recognize their unconditional love.

I was also able to see myself differently. After having spent so much intimate time with the Lord, I was able to grasp how very much He loves me. To know that no matter where I am or what I am doing, God is right there loving me, is an amazing feeling. And His love is unconditional. I cannot do anything to change how much He loves me. Once I was able to understand His love for me, I realized that I was acceptable to Him, others, and myself. I learned that other people do not determine my value. And I do not determine my value. If I do not believe that He made me beautiful, acceptable, and valuable then I am belittling what He did for me. My new found joy comes from my relationship with God. Therefore, I am in control of my happiness. I can choose to be happy by staying in close fellowship with Him, or I can be unhappy and walk away from what He has done for me. I choose the joy of the Lord.

Even when we make it our decision to choose joy, I think sometimes God gives it to us as a free gift by pouring it out on our lives. I remember the day I saw Joe after not having seen or talked with him in almost two years. It was in a public place and the meeting was purely accidental. I was speaking with someone I knew and from behind me, I heard a voice from the past. I immediately knew that voice; that voice that had called me so many names, that voice that had screamed at me and that voice that tried in its own way to say it loved me. I turned to see the person with that voice and it indeed was Joe. We both politely said hello and asked how each other was doing. We both replied we were fine and then he told me he had something of mine. I asked him what it was and he told me. I said to him if I had not needed it by now, he could just toss it. I knew in the back of my mind I actually had the item to which he was referring. I checked later at home and it was there. So I was not sure what he wanted or was trying to gain by lying to me. I was not the same person he had married. He did not know what all God had done in my life over the past two years. But I truly felt only sympathy for him. I told him good-bye and that was the end of our conversation. I walked away from him feeling totally free. I knew that I knew that I knew that he could never harm me again. He could never call me names or control me again. I sensed a strength I had never felt before. I understood then I was in control of my emotions, my responses, my handling of people and situations. But more than that, I was filled to the brim with joy. I think God poured out all the flasks of joy from heaven on me at that moment. I was so proud of myself that I had been able to speak with Joe and not be afraid of what I said or how he would react to it. I know beyond the shadow of a doubt that many of the abuses that I suffered at the hand of Joe were ones that I allowed. I enabled him to treat me in the manner he did by not taking responsibility for my own hurts and feelings from the past. I had not taken a personal inventory before I was married to see if I was as healthy as I could be. I had not allowed God to look into my life and heal the hurts that had been there for so many years. After I gave Him permission to enter in and clear out the dirt, I now had a clean heart with which I can praise Him. God had truly performed many miraculous healings in me and my interaction with Joe gave evidence to those healings. I now walked with a confidence that could have only come from Him.

Part Four: Reaching Out

You have done so much for me, O Lord.
No wonder I am glad! I sing for joy.
Psalm 92:4 (TLB).

Chapter Eighteen: Don't Waste The Pain

Comfort those who are in any trouble
with the comfort we ourselves have received from God.
2 Corinthians 1:4 (NIV).

This book has not been easy for me to write. Not because I had to relive my pain in order to put words on paper, but because I know there are so many people who are hurting just like I was. I was bound by past hurts and many of those hurts were not my choice. Things were done to me and I had no control over them. I do not believe that God brought my hurts into my life, but I believe He allowed them. I was always aware of Him in my life. Even as a child being abused, I knew He was there. When I was having difficulties with my mother and our relationship, I knew He was there. He was there when my husband was abusing me and He was there through all my years of trying to find love. Sometimes, I do not understand why He allowed me to travel the road I have traveled. But I have learned that regardless of how I felt, I can look back and see His hand was always with me. I know that is very difficult to see when one is in the middle of their pain, but it is true.

For years, I kept going through the motions of living. I was in a cycle of being hurt. But God, through classes, pastors, and individuals, showed me how I was wounded and He then gave me a choice. I could either stay in my pain, which I had grown quite comfortable with over the years, or I could reach out to Him and find healing. I had to choose to be free of my pain. God will never force anything on us. He has given us a free will, even when He knows something is good for us. We still have to choose it. So I made the choice to be free. I will never lie to anyone and say the road to healing is easy. There were many times I was hurting more than any of the abuses I had lived through. And there were many days I just wanted to lie in bed and not face the world or think about anything. But my desire to get rid of all my junk was stronger than wanting to continue to live with it. The first step is always the hardest and many battles will be thrown in your path to try and discourage you to abandon your chosen road. But I can only encourage you to stay the course. You will have to go over many obstacles before the battle is won. But the victory is so worth the fight. And if God brings you to a fight, He will see you through the fight.

I am not sure if I will ever be a lay counselor, but I do know that God used the class as an avenue to speak to me in a way that I would listen. We have to be willing to hear Him when He calls to us. Sometimes is it a still small voice and other times it is a hurricane. But either way, we must answer. I can never take credit for anything He has done in my life. And I do not want to waste the pain I went through. I have not been made comfortable just so I can feel His joy. I have to be a comfort to others. I know there are people who have experienced pains similar to or worse than mine. But I cannot share the pain others feel if I have not experienced it myself. My desire is that someone can look at me, see HIM, and want to start their healing process. There is nothing I have done to be free except be obedient and listen. We each have been given something that we are to use to help others. But if we remain bound and hurt, then someone else may miss their healing because we weren't available to them. I have a responsibility to Him to be all I can for Him. It is not that we think we can do anything of lasting value by ourselves; Our only power and success come from God (2 Corinthians 3:5 NLT)

Chapter Nineteen: HE is the Healer

Happy is he...Who says of the Lord, He is my safe place
And my tower of strength;
He is my God in whom is my hope.
Psalm 91:1-2 (BBE).

There are so many abuses in the world today, hardly anyone can escape being touched by them. The number of children that suffer sexual abuse is on the increase daily. These children will then grow up to be wounded adults and either deal with their pain, hide it away and become a dysfunctional individual, or they will mask their pain through some form of sinful or an unhealthy lifestyle. Wounds can come from so many other places than sexual abuse. We go to church every Sunday and sit next to someone who is wounded, afflicted, or addicted, and they don't know where to turn. We all put on our bright smiles and pretend we are living the perfect Christian life. We do not want others to know our faults. We don't want other to know our secret sins. We don't want others to know our hurts. I know; I did it for many years. But what is the purpose of that? Is it more important that everyone think we have it all together than it is to relieve ourselves of the hurts and injuries that only keep us from true joy? Is it more important to try and cover our sins than to experience true forgiveness and be set free from them? We are all alike. We all have hurts and we all have sins. We need to move past caring about what other people will think about us and move into what God thinks about us. Caring about people's opinions more than God's is really another form of being bound.

But many times, we do not know how to move into His healing. We cannot see past our hurts to know where to begin. I have found that the Bible can address every hurt or issue that you may have in your life. But it is a choice to seek Him out. We have to want to look at ourselves and be willing to work through our stuff in order to be like Him. We have to be willing to get real with ourselves and with Him. We must no longer want to hide behind our excuses. We have to be willing to turn to Him. First seek the counsel of the Lord (1 Kings 22:5 NIV). He already knows everything about us, so we should have no fear in telling Him we are injured or have sin. Sometimes we want to tell everyone else but Him. When we do this, we are often telling another wounded person and they, in their hurts, cannot see any way to help us. That can leave us with even more rejection and pain. If God wants you to share with someone, He will put faithful prayer warriors in your path that can cover you and not do you any more harm. We do not have to tell every member of the congregation, just Him. HE KNOWS US!!!! And more important, He STILL LOVES US! There is no fear in love. But perfect love (which is God) drives out fear (1 John 4:18 NIV). After all, He created us. For by Him were all things created, that are in heaven, and that are on earth, visible and invisible... all things were created through Him and for Him (Colossians 1:16 NIV) We simply have to cry out to Him. When I cry out to you, my enemies will turn back; This I know, because God is for me (Psalm 56:9 NIV).

Once we turn to Him, we have to trust Him. Trust in the Lord with all your heart, and lean not on your own understanding. In all your ways acknowledge Him, and He will make straight your paths (Proverbs 3:5-6 NIV). Trusting is often a very difficult step for someone who has been hurt.

But if we realize that God created us, knows everything about us, and still loves us, perhaps we can begin to trust Him. For surely I know the plans I have for you, says the Lord, plans to prosper you and not for harm, to give you hope and a future. Then when you call upon me and come and pray to me, I will listen to you. You will seek me and find me when you seek me with all you heart. (Jeremiah 29:11-13 NIV). In trusting Him, we have to remember above all else that He loves us! I am convinced that neither death, nor life, nor angels, nor rulers, nor things present, nor things to come, nor powers, nor height, nor depth, nor anything else in all creation, will be able to separate ME from the love of God in Christ Jesus our Lord (Romans 8:38-39 NRSV).

We also have to believe that He will protect us. For in the time of trouble He shall hide me in His pavilion; in the secret place of His tabernacle He shall hide me. (Psalm 27:5 NIV). The healing process is often slow and painful, but God will keep you safe and will fight the battles for you. The Lord will fight for you, and you won't need to lift a finger! (Exodus 14:14 TLB). For it is HE who shall tread down our enemies (Psalm 108:13 NIV).

We just have to follow His lead and trust in Him. And sometimes, we have to hold our peace. This is often very difficult in a battle. We want to jump ahead of God and help Him. But He does not need our help. For the battle is the Lord's (1 Samuel 17:47 NIV). We have to be able to ask ourselves the question, If God be for us, who can be against us? (Romans 8:31 NIV) And we have to believe His promise which says, Never will I leave you; never will I forsake you (Deuteronomy 31:8 NIV).

Once we realize we can trust God and know that He loves us and will protect us, we can let Him restore us. And the God of all grace, who called you to His eternal glory in Christ, after you have suffered a little while, will Himself restore you, and make you strong, firm, and steadfast. (1 Peter 5:10 NIV). He will see us through any trial that comes our way. Many times it is not about what we go through, but HOW we go through. We can ourselves sometimes determine how long we will remain in a battle. If we can learn to praise Him while we wait for Him to deliver us, the battle will go much quicker. Praise is something we all seek. Think about when you are working on a project and someone tells you what a great job you are doing. How does that make you feel? It usually makes you want to work even harder and therefore complete your project more quickly. How much more so do you think our heavenly Father desires to hear our praise? He is working on your difficult situation to bring you to a place of peace and restoration in Him. He is making a way for you where you thought there was no way. I will praise the Lord who counsels me (Psalm 16:7 NIV). Many times, we do not feel like praising Him because we cannot see Him working on our behalf. It is then that we have to, Fix our eyes not on what is seen, but on what is unseen; for what is seen is temporary, but what is unseen is eternal (2 Corinthians 4:18 NIV). God uses our daily walk to bring us closer to Him. He has made everything beautiful in its time; He has also set eternity in the hearts of men (Ecclesiastes 3:11 NIV). He only desires that we live a life full of His peace and His joy. I will heal my people and will let them enjoy abundant peace and security (Jeremiah 33:6 NIV). When we are going through our healing process, there is One thing we can be confident of, that He who began a good work in you will carry in on to completion, until the day of Christ Jesus (Philippians 1:6 NIV).

There are many avenues available today that one can use to find God's healing. Pastors, lay counselors, and teachers are equipped to help you focus on God and what He wants to do in your life. Use the resources that are available to you. If you don't know where to turn, consult with your pastor. God is the ultimate healer and will work through His people to bring healing to you. I only want to encourage you to take the first step toward your healing by turning to Him. He does not care where you have been, only where you are going. He is more than able to relieve your pain, heal your wounds, and fill you with His joy and peace. There is no other feeling like knowing He is your rock, your fortress, and your best friend. And you can never Get In so deep that God can't Get you Out!

Words to live by, my friend:
If God brings you to it, He will bring you through it.
Happy moments, Praise God
Difficult moments, Seek God
Quiet moments, Worship God
Painful moments, Trust God
Every moment, Thank God
-Author unknown

Epilogue

As I put the last word of this book on paper, I experienced both a sense of accomplishment and a sense of relief. I was relieved to have finally put my experiences on paper and was grateful to be able to give God glory for what all He had done in my life. I felt God had went through every dark corner my heart and shined His light to reveal all the things in my life that were keeping me from a closer relationship with Him. I continued to pray that I would have clean hands and a pure heart with which to worship Him.

I knew the book was ready for publishing, but I was struggling with how my mother was going to react if she were to ever read the book. I was still living in fear of her and her responses. I prayed for God's direction as to what I should do next. I knew in my heart of hearts that sharing what I had written with her had to be the next step, but it was one that I feared and began to pray that I would not have to do. I went for several months without doing anything, trying to avoid what I knew I had to do. I will admit that I even selfishly prayed for God to take her home so I would not have to share my truth with her. I did not pray that out of anger, just fear. I thought it would be the easiest way for me to handle the situation. But that would not have solved any problems and would have probably caused me more pain in the future. But that was the level of fear I had towards her.

I finally felt it was time to contact my mother and I wrote a letter to her explaining some of the hurts and abuses that I had gone through as a child, including my feelings of fear toward her. It was not a lengthy letter, but I shared what God had done in my life to heal those hurts. After writing the letter, I held on to it for a few days, asking God to stop me from mailing it if it was not His will that my mother read it.

During those days of waiting and praying, I happened to stop by the church in the middle of the day. It was at that time I experienced a divine appointment. Those occur when God wants to get something to you or say something to you and He uses other people to speak for Him. I saw someone from our praise and worship team and she told me about a service I had missed the previous week. She insisted that I get the DVD to be able to see what God had done in the service. I was excited about getting the DVD, but it was the middle of the day and the tape ministry was not open for business. But, as God would have it, the manager of the tape ministry happened to be there that day and opened the store for me to be able to buy the DVD. I eagerly purchased that DVD along with several others and headed home.

Once I was at home, I began to watch the service from the previous week. I enjoyed the praise and worship and could see that God was blessing His people that day. At one point, the pastor began to talk about people needing to make restitution in relationships. He even made the statement that some one might need to write a letter and put it in the mail. I was floored!!!!!! I felt as if my pastor were right in my living room, talking to me directly. When God wants to get a word to you, He will find a way!

I knew I had to mail that letter in spite of my fears. I put it in the mailbox the next day and began to pray that God would prepare my heart for whatever response my mother would have. I was expecting an angry one, but at same time was not trying to have any preconceived ideas about what she would say. Five days after mailing the letter, I received an email from my mother that totally shocked me. She said she was sorry for what had happened to me and that she felt she was to blame for not having seen things that were going on when I was a child. She said she loved me and not only wanted to see me, but needed to see me. I was not prepared for that type of a response and it really took me by surprise. But I was able to see the effort it had taken for her to write what she did and I could feel the pain in her voice from the words she wrote. I responded to her email, telling her I would be glad to meet with her and we set up a time for the following week.

As soon as the time to meet with my mother was arranged, I began to pray. I knew I could not go that appointment without having in me what He wanted to say. I prayed for my words to be His words and to see her through His eyes. I knew it was going to have to be His love reaching out to her because I had too much fear to reach out on my own. He had answered so many prayers before, I knew He would once again make a way for me. I told Cathy and Fern about the meeting and asked them to also pray. I asked them to not only pray for me, but to also pray for my mother. I had been dealing with many of these issues for years and she was hearing about all of them for the first time. She had a lot of information to process in a very short time. After we all agreed to pray, Fern told me she had started reading a book and that I needed to read it at some time. She had suggested books to me in the past and I usually got around to reading them. Right then, I felt I did not have time to read a book since I had a meeting to prepare for. But that would not be the case.

Fern contacted me the next day, insisting that I read the book entitled *In Every Pew Sits A Broken Heart* by Ruth Graham[5]. Fern was very firm in having me read it before I met with my mother. She was in tears as she shared portions from the book and kept insisting that it was me and that I HAD to read it. I picked it up from her that very night and gave her my word that I would read it. I do not recall having seen Fern so emotional about a book or so insistent that I do something. That was very out of character for her and her behavior reinforced my promise to her I would read the book. But I was not prepared for what I was about to read or how it would affect my world and how I saw issues and people.

The book dealt a great deal with forgiveness and forgiving people who had hurt us. I felt I had forgiven my mother, but that book helped me see that I had not. I had substituted forgiveness with walls of protection. I was able to see my part in my relationship with my mother and how I had built walls around myself to keep her and many others out. God was speaking to me through that book and I did not like what He was saying. It was too painful. I had to admit my faults and see how very high and thick my walls were. He was again giving me an opportunity to either see myself and change, or stay in my pain. But my pain at that time was very real and intense.

I called Fern in tears and sarcastically told her to never give me another book to read. I was almost angry with her because of the pain I was feeling, but I knew God had worked through her to bring me to another area where His healing so desperately needed to take place. Once again, God proved to me that when He wants to get a word to you, He will find a way to do it! My pain was growing with each chapter of the book; I did not know what to do except to crawl up into His arms and cry. But I did more that just cry. I sobbed from the depths of my soul and let go of so many hurts that I had kept buried for years. I let Him be my father, wrap His arms around me and hold me as I told Him my most intimate hurts and pains. It was not easy to admit the hurts that I myself had caused because I knew they not only hurt me, but also had hurt my relationship with my family. I might have lived in fear when I was a child, but I had taken those fears into my adult life and intensified them where my mother was concerned. I literally cried for hours, thought I was finished, and then would cry in His arms more the next day. I finally reached a point where I felt I could not cry anymore.

After draining myself of hurts and taking a good look at myself, I began to see things differently. I sensed a peace that I had not felt before and I was able to look at my mother in a way I had not before. I knew she still seemed unhappy to me, but I knew I was not responsible for that. I knew that even though our meeting would be a painful one, it would also be an honest one. I felt as if I had nothing to fear where my mother was concerned.

I went to meet my mother with a peace I never thought possible. We talked about my childhood, different family members, and how we had seen each other through the years. She said she could see a change in me. I told her it was the peace that God had given me over the past few years by healing me of my hurts. I was able to communicate honestly with my mother and I felt that within itself was a miracle. I came away knowing I no longer had to live in fear of her. I had killed another enemy and sensed a great deal of peace flow over me. We still have issues in our relationship that we are continuing to work on, but we can do it honestly. We may never have an intimate relationship, but it will be one built on honesty and honor for one another.

Once again, God had made a way for me where I had thought there would never be a way. He had opened the door to a relationship I had closed. NEVER give up on God. We cannot see with our human eyes the ways He is working on our behalf. He only requires obedience and trust in Him. Others will fail us, but He never will. I encourage you once again to trust Him and take every care to Him. He truly has all the answers!!

References:

[1] Dr. Bryan Cutshall
Senior Pastor
Twin Rivers Worship Center
St. Louis, Missouri
[2] Caring for People God's Way
The American Association of Christian Counselors
Timothy E. Clinton, Ed.D, President
PO Box 739
Forest, VA 24551
[3] Dr. Diane Langberg
The American Association of Christian Counselors
Timothy E. Clinton, Ed.D, President
PO Box 739
Forest, VA 24551
[4] Waymaker
Percy Brady
1992 Terry Cummings Music/BMI
[5] In Every Pew Sits A Broken Heart
Ruth Graham,
2004, Zondervan, ISBN 0-310-24339-4

Resources:
National Domestic Abuse Hotline 1-800-799-7233
National Sexual Assault Hotline 1-800-656-HOPE
Childhelp USA National Child Abuse Hotline
1-800-4-A-CHILD (1-800-422-4453)
Boys Town National Hotline 1-800-448-1833
National Coalition Against Domestic Violence 303-839-1852

CPSIA information can be obtained
at www.ICGtesting.com
Printed in the USA
FFOW03n1650161017
41170FF

9 781420 873931